DIRTY JOKES AND BEER
STORIES OF THE UNREFINED

DREW CAREY

DIRTY JOKES AND BEER

STORIES OF THE UNREFINED

 HYPERION NEW YORK

ISBN 0-7868-6351-X

Paperback ISBN 0-7868-8559-9

Designed by Kathy Kikkert

6 8 10 9 7 5

This book is dedicated to everyone at Hyperion for having such a tremendous amount of trust in me, considering that I've never written a book before and was kicked out of college twice.

I would dedicate this book to my mother and my family, but they haven't given me as much money as Hyperion has.

THE THANK YOU PAGE

Thank you to Bruce Helford, the Executive Producer of *The Drew Carey Show,* and the guy I created the show with, for all of your honest opinions; and your ability to say that something really sucks without coming right out and saying it.

Thank you to my managers, Rick Messina and Richard Baker, to my lawyer, Dennis Ardi (glad you're on my side), and to all of my agents at the United Talent Agency. The check's in the mail.

Thank you to my accountant, Walter Lesley, and my publicists at Wolf-Kasteler, Christina Papadopoulos and Ame Van Iden. Thank you all for fighting for me and being my friend.

Thank you to Mort Janklow, my book agent, who closed this deal while he was holed up in his bathroom with the flu. No lie.

Thank you to Marcy Woolard, my assistant. How do you put up with it? The good boss, the nice car, the easy hours?

Thank you to all the writers on *The Drew Carey Show*. Without you, what would I say? Thanks for accepting me as one of your own.

Thank you to Sam Simon, who I am lucky to count as more than just a friend, but a role model. The only way I could be as funny and as nice as you, is in my dreams.

Thank you to all my cast mates on the show: Diedrich, Ryan, Christa, Kathy, Craig, Ian, and everyone else, including my great crew. I'm the luckiest guy on the face of the earth.

Thank you for all of the last-minute editing help that I got from Les "King of the Big Dick Jokes" Firestein (punch-up and editing) and Betsy Voinovich (very helpful story note's, and much needed thought organization on some of the essay's), who both came in about five day's before the deadline and helped calm me down and show me where the apostrophe's are supposed to go.

Thank you everyone who's ever touched me, seen me, or pumped my gas. I love you all.

A NOTE TO THE READER

Thanks for taking the time to read my first book. I hope you enjoy it.

I just wanted to remind you that I didn't use a ghost writer for this. I could have. I probably should have, it would've been easier. But because of pride, I didn't. It's all mine, except for a couple of jokes that I got from my friends, and the jokes at the beginning of the chapters. So, if you're a "real writer" and you're thinking to yourself, "I could've done better than this," you're probably right. But then, you don't have a TV show, so . . . I'm sorry. I know that I only write "pretty good for a celebrity"; I am to writing what Bruce Willis is to the Blues. But I didn't make the marketplace, I just took advantage of it.

While writing this book, there were a few tools I used that I couldn't have done without: My Macintosh computer (Macs Rule!), and Microsoft Word 6.0.1 (I had Word 5.1 until just this year, and now I kick myself for not upgrading sooner). I also used two great programs, Inspiration®, and IdeaFisher®, both available at your local computer store. I couldn't have written this book without them. My biggest help, though, was from the publishers of Writer's Digest Books. I have a whole slew of "how to write" books from them that were like my own personal "English Professor on a shelf." They were full of invaluable advice, and I can't recommend books from WDB highly enough for the first-time celebrity book writer.

CONTENTS

STORIES OF THE UNREFINED

HELLO

A woman is at a bar, drinking and depressed. A man walks in and sits next to her. He, too, is drinking and depressed. After a time, the man asks the woman, "What are you so depressed about?"

She says, "My husband left me because he thought I was too kinky."

He says, "Really? My wife left me because she thought I was too kinky!"

They order another drink, and she says to him, "Hey listen, we're both adults here, and it looks like we might have a little something in common . . . *whaddya say we go back to my place and see what happens?"*

He says, "Sounds like a great idea!" And they finish their drinks and leave.

When they get to her place, she says to him, "Wait right here, I'm going to go change into something a little more comfortable." She goes to her bedroom and puts on some black leather boots with six-inch heels, a leather miniskirt, a rubber bra with the nipples cut out, a dog collar, and a leather hood. She then grabs a riding crop and some handcuffs and saunters seductively out to the living room where she sees the guy putting on his coat and hat and heading out the door.

"Where ya going?" she asks. "I thought we were going to get kinky?"

"Hey," he says, "I fucked your dog, I shit in your purse . . . I'm outta here!"

You can tell that joke a hundred different ways, but it's never as funny as when you say "fucked" and "shit" in the punch line.

Believe me, I've tried.

"I shagged your dog and spit in your purse." No.

"I had sexual relations with your dog and defecated in your purse." No.

"I blew your dog and pissed in your purse." Close, but still no cigar.

I mean, you get the same information if you don't use the dirty words, so you don't *really* need them. You just need them if you want the joke to be as funny and entertaining as it can possibly be. That's the fun of the joke—that it's ribald.

The same thing is true with this book. Yes, there are a lot of vulgarities in here and I wouldn't recommend it for small children or the easily offended. But I only left them in because I didn't think that the things I'd written would be as funny without them.

I wish, for the sake of those easily offended, that I could be as funny in some other way, but I really can't. Oh, I can get laughs if I work clean all right, no problem. Even now, I do plenty of corporate work where they want me to do a clean show and I do just fine. I just can't get enough of the kind of really *big* laughs it takes to satisfy me the way my regular vulgar act in front of a regular crowd does. I found this out years ago when I was doing nothing but my stand-up act for a living.

I started out working squeaky clean and getting respectable laughs. Then, wanting to get more road work and make more money, I started talking to the audience with the same words I used when I talked to my friends in a bar. I went from respectable laughs to belly laughs. I got more work and made more money.

After that, I even stopped censoring my subject matter and went before every crowd like they were all old drinking buddies, speaking as intimately as I cared to. Now I have my own television show and a zillion-dollar book deal.

The key to all this success wasn't the fact that I used vulgar language, though. Being vulgar just to be vulgar won't get you far. (Okay, Dice Clay sold out Madison Square Garden, and porno is a billion-dollar industry. But that's about it.) The key was, I was being honest with the audience, and true to myself. And a big part of that honesty was using common words to help make my points and to paint a clear, unmistakable picture in every audience member's mind of how I was feeling about a subject. That's the best way I know how to do things. Honest, straightforward language. And fuck me with a crooked broomstick if I'm wrong.

★ ★ ★

When the idea of doing a book originally came up, I just wanted to do a collection of short stories and nothing else. Almost immediately, my book agent nixed that idea, saying that it wouldn't sell well if it wasn't close to my "television character." (A lot of people still don't realize that my "television character" uses swear words around his buddies and dreams of having sex with cheerleaders and bikini models night and day, just like I do. He just waits until the cameras are out of his house to do it.) You see, my agent knew how much money we all could make on this deal. I didn't. I just wanted to write some funny stories.

Then I said, "Well, how about if I put in stuff about the show? Memos we've gotten from the network censor, bad reviews that we've gotten, what Mimi's really like, things like that?" I reasoned that this would make fans of the show happy, while at the same time I could still write my funny stories and get paid for it. That line of nonsense seemed to make my book agent happy enough, but then the book publishers came into the picture.

They said things like, "You know, we'd really like it if you could write chapters on things like 'Drew's Guide To Dating,' and 'Drew's Dining Tips,' and 'Drew On Beer,' stuff like that. We can even get you a ghost writer!" Silently, I thought about how I'd rather stick my face in a homeless guy's ass.

They were right, though. All the best-selling books by comics-turned-sit-com-stars were basically written-down stand-up routines as told to ghost writers who wrote it down for them and got a lot of money for it but none of the credit. The public seems to love that stuff, and who can blame them? It's funny, easier to read than the TV Guide, and rarely offensive. I would be stupid and selfish not to give the public what they want.

So, what to do? The only things we all agreed on for sure were that it shouldn't be a book about "my tragic life" (those kinds of celebrity books are both boring and full of shit), that I didn't want to use a ghost writer, and that it had to be funny.

Finally, we reached a compromise so I could become an instant millionaire.

We'll start off with "Dirty Jokes": A collection of humorous essays (although some of them are nothing but me bitching about things I don't like). They're for the editors and publishers at Hyperion. I wrote it while holding a gun to my own head. Thanks for the cash.

Then, we'll be off to "Beer": This is the "funny because it's true" section: A lot of behind-the-scenes stuff about me, my television show, and my show-biz life. I dedicate it to my literary agent, Mort. Yes, that's right. I have an agent named Mort.

(A note on the dirty jokes that start out each of these chapters: I didn't write them. Nobody knows who wrote them, or when or where. They're just bar jokes that I've heard over the course of the years, and I'm passing them along to you because I love to tell them.)

And finally, for your study hall reading pleasure, "Stories of the Unrefined": The small collection of short stories that the publishers at Hyperion wish would just go away. In fact, after reading the first two that I wrote, they started using phrases like, "Gee, these are kind of dark," and "our jobs are at stake here."

If you bought this book to find out what I'm really like when I'm not on TV, read the stories first. I'm really proud of them and would have written them for free. The rest of the book (which I'm also very proud of and think is damn funny) I just wrote for money.

In writing and planning this book, I had to make a few assumptions about you, the reader. First, I had to assume that you're buying this book because you're a fan of my stand-up act or my television show. And, I had to assume that you are like the vast majority of people in this country, in that you like a good dirty joke, and don't mind vulgar language as long as it's funny.

Then, I wrote you the best book that my minimal talent would allow. I wrote it imagining that you were sitting with me in a bar, and that we've decided to stay up all night getting drunk together. The jukebox is going to play nothing but our favorite songs, and I'm buying. And then, if we're still awake when daylight comes, we're all going to call in sick to work.

Sounds like fun already, doesn't it?

DIRTY JOKES

VEGAS

There's a guy who lives in Ohio. One morning, he hears a voice in his head. The voice says, "Quit your job, sell your house, take all your money, and go to Las Vegas."

He ignores the voice.

Later in the day, he hears the voice again. "Quit your job, sell your house, take all your money, and go to Las Vegas."

Again, he ignores the voice.

Soon he hears the voice every minute of the day. "Quit your job, sell your house, take all your money, and go to Las Vegas."

He can't take it anymore. He believes the voice. He quits his job, *sells his house, takes all his money, and flies to Las Vegas. As soon as he steps off the plane, the voice says, "Go to Caesar's Palace."*

He goes to Caesar's Palace.

The voice says, "Make your way to the roulette table."

He goes to the roulette table.

The voice says, "Put all your money on red 23."

He puts all his money on red 23.

The dealer spins the wheel. It comes up black 17.

The voice says, "Fuck."

I've been living in or visiting Las Vegas since I was nineteen years old. It's my second-favorite city in the world, next to Cleveland. Gambling, babes, booze . . . all the great things in life are there, twenty-four hours a day.

Oh, and if you get up in time after a night of boozing, throwing dice, and chasing skirts, you can also catch some of that fabulous sunshine that Las Vegas is famous for.

The best thing about Las Vegas is that no one pretends to be responsible for your behavior like they do in the rest of the country. There's no meddling self-righteous liberals or right-wing Christian demagogues telling you that you can't do something fun with your own time and money. If you can afford it, it's yours. Sex, gambling, drugs, Sigfried and Roy . . . they're all there for the taking.

And, it beats the pants off of Atlantic City. I guess Atlantic City is okay if you can't afford to fly to Nevada, but man . . . don't even try to compare the two. It's no contest.

Las Vegas has sexy showgirls in bikinis hanging out by the pool. Atlantic City has old ladies in parkas with buckets full of nickels, bitching their way through the casinos screaming, "Where's my bus? I have a coupon! What can I get for free?"

There really is an inordinate amount of old people in Atlantic City. During the weekdays it's like a retirement village. Nothing against old people, mind you. It's just that in Atlantic City they're so damn s-l-l-o-o-o-w. Ever get stuck walking behind old people in a crowd? No matter how hard you try you can't get around them. Jump to the left, they lean left. Juke to the right, they lean right. Then, out of nowhere, they'll just stop. It's like they have a sixth sense about getting in people's way. They should be guarding Jordan.

A hundred people standing behind them with someplace to go, and they stop right in their tracks, like their batteries went dead. Like the guy decided, "I tell ya, Marge, all my life it's been left, right, left. Well, the hell with it. I'm not walking anymore. Let them come to me."

Besides cranky old people who jam up the aisles, Atlantic City is also home to the friendliest people in the world. What a giving, helpful breed those Atlantic City folks are.

They'll spend all day playing quarter machines, the most popular type of slot machine in Atlantic City. Quarter after quarter after quarter tossed down a metal tube so they can spin three wheels and see pictures of some fruit. They don't even want to win half the time, they just want to get rid of their quarters.

Then, they'll go out to the boardwalk, see some poor guy who's starving, with nothing to eat, nowhere to sleep . . . "Got a quarter?" he'll ask politely.

"Go fuck yourself," says the friendly Atlantic City tourist, holding his bucket of quarters close to his body. "This is my gambling money."

A friend of mine sums it up best. He said that the difference between Las Vegas and Atlantic City is the difference between getting conned by a beautiful call girl and getting mugged by a crack head.

*   *   *

Las Vegas is known for its stupendous stage shows. Many of these shows feature trained animals. Now, God knows I'm no animal rights nut, but there's one thing that sickens me about animals being on stage entertaining a showroom full of Vegas tourists.

The trainer will have the animals jumping through fire, doing flips, sitting up . . . you know, really putting on a show. And then, the *trainer* takes the *bow*!

To me, that's like having Eddie Van Halen's guitar teacher come out at the end of one of his shows. "Thank you, I'm responsible for everything you saw here tonight! Thank you!"

Since first seeing this phenomenon, every time I see an animal that attacks a trainer on one of those TV specials, I think, "Well, no wonder. The Supremes should've done something like that to Diana Ross a long time ago."

When I'm in Las Vegas, the Hard Rock Hotel and Casino is one of my favorite places to stay (along with Caesar's, and everywhere else I perform. Or anyplace that gives me a free room). It's off the strip, packed with great-looking men and women, small enough to not get lost in, and across the street from a first-class strip club. Add to that the constant blaring of great rock and roll music throughout the casino (even in the elevators and underwater in the pool!), and you really can't go wrong. You'll feel young and horny the whole time you're there.

The Hard Rock also has the most pandering corporate slogan I've ever heard: "Save the Planet." You can't get away from it. It's on every sign, every chip, every matchbook. "Save the Planet." Like you can really save the planet from people in the first place, and if you wanted to, you could do it by drinking and gambling at the Hard Rock. "Hey, not only am I getting shit-faced drunk and picking up cute chicks, I'm saving the planet!"

And what the hell does it mean, "Save the Planet"? Save what planet? How? Who? Why? When? What will it cost me? There's no pamphlets at the door, no nothing.

Save the Planet. Scramble the eggs. Burn the toast.

Every time I play craps there, when I roll the dice I yell "Save the Planet!" Then, win or lose, I loudly announce, "I don't care if I win or not, I just want the planet to be safe," while I count my hundred-dollar chips. This usually brings a tear to the eyes of the environmentally sensitive pit bosses and stickmen who work there.

Maybe they think that the slogan will take the sting out of losing your money there. "Hey, it's okay. Hopefully, some of this money will go toward saving the planet." I'm surprised that losing there isn't tax deductible.

If you ever find yourself at the Hard Rock Hotel and Casino in Las Vegas, ask one of the bartenders or card dealers what you can personally do to make the planet a safer place. But wait until they're really busy. Then interrupt them and ask, "Excuse me, miss, but how can I do more to save the planet right now?" Believe me, they won't mind. Concern for the planet is better than a tip at the Hard Rock!

Once, I stumbled upon what I thought was the real reason the "Save the Planet" slogan exists. Concrete, irrefutable proof that the Hard Rock Casino really cares. There's a row of slot machines off in the corner of the casino with a counter above them, spinning down the acres of rain forest left in the world. At first, it looks like another row of mega-jackpot machines, but then when you read the fine print you discover their real altruistic purpose. They're not there to take your money.

They're there to Save the Planet! I think that they reset it every so often just so they don't look stupid when it gets down to zero after a week.

They claim that a "portion" of the proceeds from those machines will go directly to help save the rain forest. Of course, no one ever plays them. They're busy saving the planet in some other way, like playing video poker, or "accidentally" grabbing someone's ass.

Maybe the Hard Rock could rework the roulette tables so that every time someone wins on a red number, they don't get the money. They send the person's winnings directly to the hut of some poor family in the rain forest. Or if you get a blackjack, the rain forest wins! What do *you* need the money for, you greedy prick? What's the matter? Don't you care about the environment?

And why only the rain forests? Is that all we need to do to save the whole planet? What about the deserts and the oceans? What about Bosnia or South Central LA? Why do only the rain forests get all of the "Save the Planet" money?

I wonder how much of the planet has actually been saved since the first Hard Rock opened its doors to the public? After all, there's Hard Rock restaurants all over the world. I guess the planet must be pretty safe by now, wouldn't you? (Except for the trees that were chopped down to build more Hard Rocks, that is. All of their bars are made of the nicest wood. . . .) When can we stop saving the planet? I must write the Hard Rock and ask them that. "Dear Hard Rock, just for my records, how close are we to finally saving the planet? And, once it's safe, will you be changing your corporate slogan to reflect the planet's saved state? Like 'We Saved the Planet,' or 'If It Weren't for Our Hamburgers the Planet Would Be Dead Right Now'?"

Meeting eager-to-please, open-minded sex partners seems to

be the main activity at the Hard Rock Hotel and Casino. On the weekends, it even ranks higher than gambling. How that helps to save the planet I don't know, but I'm all for it. "Hey baby, sit on my face and save the planet."

A more appropriate slogan for the Hard Rock would be "Get Laid and Gamble." It would even look better on all those T-shirts that tourists line up for an hour to buy. Say it out loud for me. "Get Laid and Gamble." There. Doesn't that make you want to go there and spend your money more than a silly slogan like "Save the Planet"?

As much as I hate a slogan that's as vague and obsequious as "Save the Planet," at least it's a more endearing corporate slogan than something like, "Fuck You, Give Us Your Money."

Hey! Maybe they could use that for Atlantic City. "Welcome to Atlantic City—Fuck You, Give Us Your Money."

It would be the first honest slogan in America.

BASIC HOME THEATER

A guy buys a big 200-acre ranch out in the country. One day, shortly after he moves in, he's relaxing on his front porch when a pickup truck comes rambling down the one dirt road to his house and screeches to a halt in front of him.

"Howdy neighbor!" the pickup driver says. "My name's Bill! I live next door and wanted to welcome you to the neighborhood!"

"Well, thanks Bill. That's right friendly," says the man.

"My pleasure," Bill says. Then, "Hey listen, the reason I drove over here is that I'm having a party this Saturday and I'd really like you to come. And it is sure going to be a doozy. There's going to be *eatin', and drinkin', and fuckin', and fightin' . . . I tell you, it's going to be great!"*

"Well, that sounds just fine, Bill," says the man. "What should I wear?"

"Oh, it don't matter," Bill explains. "It's just gonna be you and me."

The first thing I did with my first paycheck from my first TV show (*The Good Life*, on NBC) was buy a big-screen TV.

At the time, it seemed like the most sensible purchase I could make. Of course, I had no money in the bank and my furniture was so ratty that even my stoner friends wouldn't sit in it, but who cared? A person could live without money or furniture; they can't live without a TV.

I started out small, with a thirty-five-inch Mitsubishi, from the same company that made Kamakaze aircraft in World War II. That's about the smallest you can get and still call it a big screen. I was only in a modest apartment then, so it took up the whole wall and looked huge when you walked in. I also wear my underwear a size smaller than I need to.

Of course, my television was made in Japan. All the good televisions are. The Japanese are great at making televisions, and it's darn near impossible to buy a TV that *isn't* made there. If there's a decent television brand that's still made in America, I sure can't think of it. If you know of a company that makes one, write them and tell them to advertise it once in a while.

Students in Japan also beat the heck out of American kids in important areas like science, and math, and not acting like an idiot in public. That's because American kids, instead of studying, would rather spend their time in front of television sets that are made in, er . . . Japan.

I added to the thirty-five-inch Japanese Mind Bomb a set of the four cheapest speakers I could find (made in China), and connected it to the AUX part of my stereo tuner to get almost-realistic surround sound. Not as fancy as I wanted, and I worried that I would somehow be cheating my friends out of an important part of the home theater experience when they heard it. But believe me, when I turned it up loud enough, none of my stoner friends even noticed. In fact, in between bites of my potato chips, they complimented me on the clarity of the sound.

The first movie I rented to watch on it was *Ben Hur*, and let me tell you, it was fantastic. Believe me, nothing looks better on a big TV screen with Almost-Surround Sound than the homosexual give and take between Tony Curtis and Charlton Heston.

I've been watching a lot of old movies lately. That way, I don't have to see all of that annoying product placement stuff that they do nowadays. And it's always done so obtrusively. Yeah, like I always hold my Pepsi with the label out so the camera can see it.

That's Pepsi. The Choice of a New Generation.

Another thing that I started doing quite a bit of since I got my first big screen is playing Sega Genesis. I cannot beat one game on my Sega Genesis machine. On my old Nintendo, I could beat a couple of them, but not Sega Genesis. It's impossible, and I refuse to upgrade to a faster, smarter machine because of it. I'm not blaming the machine, mind you. I don't get mad at it, or throw things at the TV when I get frustrated.

But if I ever meet the guy who invented Sega Genesis, I'm going to beat the living shit out of him.

When *The Drew Carey Show* was renewed for a second season, the first thing I did, believe it or not, was something sensible. I bought a house. The place had been a rental for many years and needed a lot of small repairs, new landscaping, and a coat of paint inside and out.

So instead of doing all that, I went out and bought a bigger TV. I knew that nothing would impress my friends more, and I was right. I've spent thousands on landscaping, paint, and draperies since then, and all they talk about when they come over is how great the TV is.

My sink constantly backs up, half the lightbulbs in the house are burned out, and my toilet runs every ten minutes like it was busted by a Swiss watchmaker. Not a word from my friends, though. As long as I have a cool TV, I might as well live in a cave. In fact, I like to think of my house as nothing more than a glorified console for my television; the ultimate stereo cabinet.

The new set was a sixty-one-inch Sony XBR. It looked great in the room with the peeling paint and burnt-out lightbulbs. I also bought a set of B&W THX speakers, a brand new Super-VHS VCR, and a top-of-the-line laser disc player.

It's more than a person needs, really, but what isn't? If we weren't all a bunch of vain gluttonous pigs, we'd be happy with nothing but bland food, plain-looking clothes, and adequate shelter. Then where would we be? Communist China, that's where, making cheap speakers for Americans, watching propaganda films on a twelve-inch, black-and-white screen and driving a Chinese version of the K-car. I shudder at the thought.

Americans don't want plain and simple and adequate. Neither does anybody in any country with money. We all want bigger and better and more. And not only that, it has to have a name that makes it sound like more than it is. That's why it's not called "a big-ass TV and some overpriced speakers" in the electronics store ads. Who would put down their hard-earned dough for something like that? Instead, they always give their products some sexy name and add unneccesary letters that remind you of sex. The "SX," for example. How many times have you seen that on an expensive electronic product (or a car)? Why not the "BJ," or the "69"? Or, better yet, the "SX BJ 69." I'd buy that, no matter what it was. "The All-New Dog Shit SX BJ 69." Give me two!

That's why it's never just a TV set and some speakers. It's a "Home Theater System."

Imagine, an actual theater in your own home. Don't we all dream of something like that at one time or another? Something so wasteful and unnecessary that we just have to have it? Like a Jaguar, or a Rolls-Royce, or two girlfriends?

The concept of a home theater is way up near the top of the pyramid as far as good old American conspicuous consumption is concerned. I mean, we already have theaters in America. Great ones, in fact. But to enjoy them we have to sit next to smelly strangers who might dress differently than we do, or might want to actually talk to us. Ick.

Instead, thanks to a happy step forward in corporate Darwinism, public theaters will soon become a thing of the past, like carpooling and mass transit. Now, we will have our own private home theaters. Good-bye expensive popcorn! Good-bye having to have our parents drop us off at the mall in the snow! Now, when the floor is sticky, I'll know exactly how it got that way.

We have our *own individual* theaters now.

It used to be just "the living room," but not anymore. With a big-enough screen and loud-enough speakers, it's a cineplex. Throw in a personal computer, a job you can do from home, and some mail-order catalogs, and you could probably live the rest of your life without coming in contact with another living human. Ever. Real Utopia at last, just like the book of Revelations promised us.

Of course, for those of you who might get homesick for the mall theater experience every now and again, maybe the Japanese could add some "crowd noise" buttons onto the remote. I suggest "Crying Baby," "Obnoxious Teenagers," and "People Who Yell At the Screen."

(When I first started making "TV money," I bought only one other stupid and unnecessary thing: an eighty-dollar laser pointer that I saw in a catalog. I don't know what I was thinking, but it seemed like a cool thing to have at the time. You know, it's a light. You point to things with it. It's made in America. I use it to mess with people's cats.)

Although having all of this equipment is really cool, it is also really expensive. More than really expensive. Ridiculously expensive. So to justify the expense, I told myself that I was going to buy and rent nothing but the finest that Hollywood had to offer: Academy Award-winning documentaries, THX-enhanced director's cut editions, and the best sensitive foreign films and dramas from the Sundance Film Festival.

You know what I watch the most of? Titty movies and porn.

What a waste of money this TV is when I'm watching that stuff. It's like paying five grand for fine china, and then not eating anything off of it but macaroni and cheese.

There's only one thing that's bad about having a big-screen TV, and that's the fact that everyone wants to come over and use it. It's worse than having a pool or a good-looking girlfriend. And if you say no, you're a prick. It really chips away at the dream of a life without human interaction.

And if you thought people talked a lot at the movies at the mall, hoo-boy. Wait till they're watching a movie with you on a TV in your own home. Yakity, yakity, yakity. And good luck getting them to leave, because unlike a movie at the mall, TV is never over.

Other than that it's the greatest. Buy a big-screen as soon as you can, and be sure it's at least a thirty-five-incher. Then get your speakers and cable hooked up and enjoy the show. And don't worry about little things like furniture. If I can live without it, so can you.

HOW TO PICK UP GIRLS

A comedian is sitting at the bar of the local comedy club on a Friday night. A beautiful woman sits next to him and says, "I saw you perform tonight, and I think that you're the funniest guy I've ever seen. I want to take you back to my house to give you the hottest, kinkiest, best night of sex you've ever had."

The comedian looks at her and says "Um . . . did you see the first show, or the second show?"

* * *

I am so mad. You know what I just found out? You know that song from the seventies, "It Ain't the Meat, It's the Motion"? Well, it's the meat.

I'm going to add that to the list of mistaken beliefs I've had about women throughout my life. Size Matters. I should carve it into my forehead so I don't forget.

You know what made me think it didn't all this time? That stupid song. I used to hear it on the radio and think to myself, "See, Drew? It's okay to be average! It's not the meat! It's the motion!" Whatever the motion was.

I remember my first year of nonvirginity trying desperately to figure out what the motion was, varying my thrusting technique every five seconds or so like a rhumba dancer who was being electrocuted.

This was while I was in college during the seventies. A great time to get laid, the seventies. No AIDS. No condoms necessary if the girl was on the pill. And, if you were lucky, no last names! Booze, pot, early Aerosmith, and easy sex. I'm telling you, I was in paradise.

Of course, as much as I thought I was getting laid in the seventies, everybody else was getting laid more. My idea of an orgy was using more than one magazine.

It's been like that all my life, really. Even now that I'm on TV. Oh, I get plenty of dates now that I have a show, and with stunningly beautiful women. But the rest of it is just about the same as it was for me in high school and college.

In high school, I was in the marching band, so you know the babes were all over me. Especially when I wore my band uniform. Not only did I look like an army colonel in one of those fake European countries they would make up for a Marx Brothers movie, I looked like an army colonel holding a trumpet.

My physique didn't help either. I wasn't allowed to drink beer yet, so I was skinny, and only weighed 123 pounds when I graduated. I guess I could've had a better body if I had liked gym class more, but I hated taking the showers afterward. I would stand there all bummed out thinking, "Man, everybody here's got hair except me." Of course, thanks to God's great sense of humor, I now have hair everywhere on my body, even inside my nose.

I rarely dated in high school, and never even made out with a girl until I got to college. But once I started, I couldn't get enough. I read every issue of *Playboy* and *Oui* (a classy magazine in those days) looking for tips on how to be a better lover and how to make myself more attractive to women. I read the *Forum* letters in *Penthouse* thinking that I could learn from them. I remember thinking sometimes when I was having sex, "Let's see now. How did 'Surprised In Cincinnatti' do it?"

Like almost every guy at that stage of his sexual development (the "I-just-got-laid-for-the-first-time" stage), I believed everything women told me about sex and sexual manners. If a *Playboy* Playmate said in her questionnaire that she liked guys in tight pants, I would go out and buy some tight pants. If she said she liked well-endowed men with big muscles and hairy chests, I would cry.

One time, a college girl I had been flirting with at a bar complimented me on my cologne. It wasn't a big compliment, she just mentioned it in passing.

"What's that you're wearing?" she asked, not even looking my way.

"Brute," I answered.

"Oh, I like Brute," she said, getting up to leave.

I thought that I had heard a secret key to scoring with women. "Ah ha!" I thought. "Chicks dig Brute!"

Within a week, I was Brute Man. When I was getting ready to go out and meet women, I would shower with Brute shampoo and Brute soap-on-a-rope. Then, after slathering my armpits with Brute antiperspirant and deodorant, I would shake Brute cologne all over my body like it was holy water. That done, I dusted my private areas with Brute talcum powder, and as the cherry topping, I would slip into a teeny pair of nylon Brute bikini underwear with a mesh pouch. Snug and secure, I would blow-dry my feather-cut disco hair, and spray it into a helmet with Brute hairspray.

I reeked.

All because some college girl remarked in passing, "I like Brute."

You should've seen me at the local disco. Helmet hair, tight bell-bottoms, platform shoes, shirt undone, gold chains. The sweet smell of Brute wafting across the dance floor like an Iranian chemical weapon. "Gee, how come I'm not getting laid more?" I wondered. "After all, I'm wearing Brute. Women can't resist it!"

No wonder my friends always wanted to open the windows when we drove anywhere.

There is one thing I learned about women back in college that is still true to this day: Women that are borderline good-looking always have an ugly friend with them when they go out to make them look even better. Wherever there's a Mary, you'll find a Rhoda. Really beautiful women hardly ever use this trick, preferring to stick to their own kind. But if a women has a few flaws, she'll find a friend with even more flaws to draw the negative attention away from her. (Sometimes men use this same trick. I know this because I once went drinking with Matthew Perry.)

Personally, I don't think that ugly people should be treated that way. Not for free anyway. If you're ugly, and your almost-pretty good-looking friend calls you up to go to a club, charge them fifty dollars.

After college, I hit a major dry spell. Not only could I not get laid, I couldn't even get strippers to take my dollar. I also discovered pornography, going to one dirty bookstore so much that they named a booth after me. I switched to Old Spice.

During my drives back and forth between the strip clubs and the porno shops, I wondered why people talked about nymphomania like it was a bad thing, and if it counted as a multiple orgasm if you added them up over the course of a week.

Every time there was an article in the paper about sex, I would turn right to it, thinking that maybe it held the key to sexual happiness that I longed for. One article said that to make sex more enjoyable you should take pain relievers about an hour before you start. Pain relievers?

Not the kind of sex I like to have, you don't. The only way I'd need a pain reliever to enjoy sex is if all of my fantasies came true at the same time.

Besides, when is someone like me ever going to know an hour beforehand that he's going to be having sex? "Let's see, the bar closes at one-thirty and there's a lot of drunk girls here, so that means that I should take two aspirins around one, one-fifteen . . ."

Making love to music was another suggestion I heard about. Unfortunately, when I got my chance, I did it to a polka. Not only was it over much too quickly, but I had to spend a week at my chiropractor's. I've avoided chubby Eastern European women ever since.

Later on, I still had no clue, and it only got worse. I had a beer belly, no hair, and less money. But that was nothing compared to when I told women that I was a comedian.

In fact, the only thing that half a life of getting laid less than half as much as the average guy has given me is jokes for my act.

Thanks to years of frustration, I have it in me to think up such gems as:

> *The last woman I had sex with just hated me. I could tell by the way she asked for the money.*

Or,

> *I'm not a good lover, but at least I'm fast.*

Or even,

> *I'm not good in bed. Hell, I'm not even good on the couch.*

Killer, huh?

After all this, what advice can I give to the Young Man of Today? Someone who might benefit from all my experience?

Nothing, pal. I still have no idea about what I'm doing when it comes to women. Maybe, avoid cheap cologne and cheesy bikini underwear. Don't expect sex on the first date, and never pay more than twenty dollars for a lap dance.

Other than that, you're on your own.

SNOWBOUND

An old man and an old woman are getting ready for bed. Suddenly, the old woman leaps out of the bathroom, and throws her bathrobe open in front of the old man.

"Super Pussy!" she yells.

The old man says, "I'll have the soup."

You don't know what humiliation is until you've shown up on your first day of junior high in moon boots and a snow suit that your mother got on sale during the summer. I looked like a demented astronaut.

I was even wearing a hat, which I found out quickly was the uncoolest thing to do, no matter how cold and windy it got. You see, I went to junior high in the early seventies, and everyone was starting to blow-dry their hair. So the last thing they wanted to do after all that work in front of the mirror with their mom's blow-dryer was to put a stocking cap over it and flatten it down. Dorks that wore hats, like me, had them snatched from their heads and tossed around the school yard in a cruel game of keep-away.

So there everyone would stand: Outside in the icy, bitter wind, waiting for the doors of Mooney Junior High to fling open; freezing to death, but with perfect hair. Because it was frozen.

Jean jackets were also very big in the winter. Jean jackets, tennis shoes (never wear galoshes!) and big combs sticking out of your back pocket. Anything that didn't protect you from the elements was a cool thing to wear. Frostbite was the ultimate status symbol.

I remember walking home from high school after wrestling practice with *wet* hair, and no cap, because I didn't want anyone to think I was stupid. Icicles would form on my head. My nostrils would freeze open. I didn't care. What if a cute girl drove by with her parents?

Then, when I would get home, I would barely be able to work the key into the door because of the onset of hypothermia. As soon as I could manage it, I would grab my grandfather's old army blanket and put it over my head like a tent while I squatted over the register.

I never looked very cool that way, but as long as someone

from school doesn't see you, cool kind of goes out the window when your life is at stake.

Every winter, you hear that song "Walking in a Winter Wonderland." But you never hear a song about how great it is to *drive* in the winter.

> *Horns honk, are ya listenin'?*
> *Across three lanes, I'm a spinnin'*
> *I caused a big fuss*
> *When I sideswiped a bus*
> *Driving in a winter wonderland.*
> *By tomorrow they will file a lawsuit.*
> *I'll be hearing from the lawyer Brown . . .*

Last winter, I actually did spin across three lanes while I was driving in Cleveland on I-480. I was only doing about twenty-five mph because the freeway was full of icy, packed snow. Then I tapped the brake pedal. Just a tap. And *bam*! There I went, spinning across three lanes and heading for the cement divider, my insurance agent flashing before my eyes. Luckily, I didn't hit anything and was able to continue on my way, clutching the steering wheel and crying like a little girl.

I think that if anyone bothered to take a survey, they would find a sharp decline in atheism during the winters in Cleveland, Ohio. I know that I said, "Oh, Jesus!" and, "Oh my God! Oh my God!" several times in the few seconds it took me to spin out.

But it's not just the roads in Cleveland that cause problems in the winter. It's the machines that they use to clear the roads. In Cleveland, if da snowplow don't get you, da salt truck will.

I can't count the number of times I've been parked in the

street and had to shovel my car out of ten feet of dirty snow after it was plowed under by the city as they cleared the center of the road for people with garages. (Okay, technically, we had a garage. But it was always so full of junk that I couldn't fit the car into it. And I couldn't park in the driveway because I never felt like shoveling it.)

Then, after all the back-breaking work I did to dig myself out, the car would be pelted by the salt truck as it made its way down the street. It always sounded like a thousand delinquent school kids throwing pebbles at you at the same time.

That's why so many people in Cleveland look for a "Winter Car." A Winter Car is a beater that you only need to last until the third week of baseball season. (That's usually when winter ends in Cleveland. Some opening day games in Cleveland have actually been called on account of snow.) Your beater can be ugly, foreign, and have only an AM radio with one speaker, as long as the rear defroster works and it has snow tires.

People in Los Angeles, which is where I live most of the year now, have no idea what I'm talking about when I mention a Winter Car. The only thing that's close to a Winter Car in LA is when someone has a second car that they wouldn't mind parking in front of a check-cashing store.

When I was a "student" at Kent State University, one of the favorite winter activities was writing your name in the snow while you were peeing. (Followed in order by sex, drinking, making snow angels, and studying.)

That's the one area where men have it all over women. Women control sex, they get the better end of the deal in a divorce, and are hardly ever in as much danger as men are during a war. But so what? Men can write their names in the snow with their pee.

That is, they can write their first names. If they're short. I mean, if your name is "Bartholomew," you're just going to write "Bart." No one wants to keep drinking pitchers of beer just to come back and put their full name in the snow. It's always "Bob" or "Pete." It's never "Anthony Rodriguez Popoudopolous III."

No matter how many people die from living in it, driving in it, or shoveling it, there's one great thing about snow that no one will deny: It can cancel school.

I remember, if there was a bad snowstorm outside, I would plant myself in front of the TV, praying that our school district would come across the bottom of the screen. I would even get up early to find out if I could go back to sleep because school was canceled. Having your school closed because of snow was the greatest feeling in the world.

If you didn't grow up around snow, I can help you imagine what it would be like. Imagine if the boss called you one morning and said, "Hey, you're sick, don't come into work."

You'd say, "But I feel great! Never better!"

And the boss would say, "Nonsense. You're sick. Stay home."

Now wouldn't that feel great? You could get errands done that you were putting off, clean out the basement . . . or you could do what I used to do when school was canceled because of snow: lie around and watch TV.

There was never anything good on, but I didn't care. I watched reruns of *The Beverly Hillbillies, Bewitched, Branded,* and every game show I could find. Then I'd watch the Prize Movie, and then Merv Griffin came on. Why go to school when you can get an education like that at home?

Back then, if I could've jumped into the TV and lived in any

TV show, it would've been *The Beverly Hillbillies*. Man, I'd rule that house. Granny making me vittles, Jethro running my errands, and Ellie Mae . . . oh, sweet Ellie Mae. Of course, I'd have to kill Uncle Jed to get to her, but so what?

I'd be in Californee, naked with Ellie Mae in the Cee-ment pond, and away from all that damn snow.

HAIL TO THE CHIEF

A man runs into a bar and says to the bartender, "Give me twenty shots of your best single-malt scotch, quick!"

The bartender pours the shots, and the man drinks them down, one at a time, as fast as he can.

The bartender says, "Wow. I never saw anybody drink that fast."

The man says, "Well, you'd drink that fast if you had what I have."

The bartender says, "Oh my God. What is it? What do you have?"

The man says, "Fifty cents."

* * *

I'm a comedian, you know. That's how I started in show business, and that's what I'll always be, long after the lovable TV Drew is dead or lives on in syndication. Comedians make fun of presidents. And their families. That's because next to popes, presidents are the ultimate sacred cows. That's my only excuse for doing this. It's an irresistible primal urge.

So to all the presidents or their families who might read this (yeah, fat chance): nothing personal. I'm just doing my job. Laugh, and the world laughs with you.

You lying sons of bitches.

Ronald Reagan has Alzheimer's disease. He's always had Alzheimer's disease. Ever since Iran-contra.

Does he seriously expect anyone to believe that he didn't know what Oliver North was up to? Bullshit.

Bullshit, bullshit, bullshit.

I didn't even mind that he did it. Arms for hostages. Sounded like a great plan. Something out of a Le Carré novel. But don't lie about it.

And thanks for all the national debt, peckerhead. Glad it helped make you popular.

"We need to balance the budget!" Oh, really? Then why didn't you? Nancy's astrologer didn't think it was the right time? Jupiter wasn't in line with Venus, or some other such New Age crap you let her use to help run the country? Did Nancy ever dress in a turban and throw chicken bones around the Oval Office to help you decide what to have for lunch?

Maybe it was because the Star Wars program was so expensive. By the way, whatever happened to that? Didn't you get us to spend billions of dollars for it? Where the fuck is it? I know that the Russians aren't much of a threat anymore, but so what? People drive Porsches when a Honda will do. Where the fuck is our billion-dollar, Russian-zapping Porsche?

I will give Reagan credit for keeping the military stakes so high with Russia that to compete with us, they ruined their economy and their whole system collapsed. Thanks. (Although, now I'm scared of pesky little countries like Azerbaijan, not to mention every disgruntled Russian scientist with a nuclear bomb for sale.)

That is, I'll give his staff credit for ruining Russia. They were the brains of the outfit, if you ask me. Sometimes I think that the whole Reagan administration was like one of those movies where they would find a guy who looks just like the president, teach him how to act like the president, and then kill the real president.

Also, I was in the marines during the Reagan years, and any presidential look-alike that beefs up the military is a-okay with me.

The entire collapse of the Bush era can be summed up in six words: "Read My Lips, No New Taxes." I bet you hear those words in your sweat-drenched nightmares, don't you George?

The American public didn't seem to mind that he lied about his involvement in the Iran-contra scandal, even though he was at all the meetings. Even though he used to be the head of the Central Intelligence Agency, so you *knew* he knew about everything that everybody did everywhere. I'm sure he still got the newsletter.

And they loved him for taking the lead on the Gulf War. Thanks for keeping our gas prices low, low, low. Thanks for making Kuwait safer than South Central LA. I hope to vacation there someday. Thanks for not killing Sadaam when you had the chance. I had five minutes about Sadaam in my act and didn't want to lose it.

But oh, Jesus, did they hate you over "Read My Lips." It's too bad you didn't say it while you were head of the CIA. You could've claimed it was some kind of secret code that meant, "A Chicken In Every Pot."

But what did we expect from a guy that let himself get pushed around by the Democratic Congress on budgetary issues worse than Reagan did. After all, raising taxes wasn't his idea, he just went along with it like some idiot.

(I can't, in good conscience, blame only presidents for this country being in such out-of-control debt. I blame Congress, mostly, because they're the only ones that are constitutionally allowed to spend money. But it doesn't help when president after president lets them get away with it without having at least some of them secretly assassinated.)

Clinton. Where to start with the lyingest, bullshittingest, most insincere misrepresenter to ever hold the office?

Didn't inhale, didn't waggle his dick at Paula Jones, wasn't greedy during the eighties, only wants to help, feels your pain, never did a line of blow, has a plan for every problem in your life no matter how small it is.

Bullshit.

Bullshit, bullshit, bullshit.

He didn't inhale because he was stupid and didn't know how. He wanted to get high, he just couldn't figure out the complicated respiratory trick that even your average crack head can do.

He doesn't remember shaking his trouser snake at Paula Jones, because he probably did it so many times to so many women that she got lost in the shuffle. He's willing to (as of this writing, anyway) donate some $600,000 that she's asking for to a charity to settle the case, but he didn't do it. And Michael Jackson never molested a little boy.

Everything he says to us sounds like some practiced pick-up line that you'd hear from some old guy trying to get laid in a disco.

"I feel your pain, baby. Let's go back to my place."

"Hi, I'm the education president. Nice tits."

He needed to raise all our taxes to get back at the rich people who were so greedy during the awful Reagan-Bush years. (Remember the Reagan-Bush years? How terrible things were?) I think that in my best year during Reagan-Bush I made just over thirty thousand. In 1989, the last year of the so-called "Decade of Greed" I was living out of my car trying not to put a bullet through my head. And then soon as Clinton gets elected and I just start to make good money, he wants to raise my taxes to get back at me.

Well, fuck you.

What were you and your wife doing in the eighties, huh? Living off the land? No, you prick, you and your lawyer wife were doing sweetheart land deals and trading in pork futures and trying to get rich like every other yuppie.

You even sent your daughter to an exclusive private rich-kid school. Nice going, especially since you're so vigorously opposed to school vouchers which would let the average Joe provide the same opportunities to his daughter that you gave to yours.

The education president, my ass. Public schools in America suck. You said as much yourself when you wouldn't send your own daughter to one. You think she'd be going to Stanford if she went to a public school in D.C.? She'd be lucky to be going to a decent community college right now. Instead of being a doctor, her goal would be to read at an eighth-grade level.

You and your "Mandate for Change." You never got more than half of the popular vote. You didn't get elected by a landslide, you fell through the cracks.

I've had it with all these assholes. Every election I have to hold my nose to vote. The way they go on and on, taking credit for things they didn't do, blaming the other party for every bad thing that no one has control over, making promises they have no intention of keeping just because a poll told them the public wanted to hear it , . .

And they always have a plan for solving every problem. Poverty, Crime, AIDS; you name it, and Big Brother can solve it right from his Ivory Tower in Washington, D.C. Call a press conference, give a speech, appoint a committee: problem solved as far as any president is concerned. On to the next problem.

For example, while I was writing this chapter, Big Brother Bill gave a "major speech" in California about racism. What he said was that racism is bad, he was against it, and if we all just worked together a little harder, we could get rid of it.

Race problem solved. Congratulations. Better put on your lab coat and get to work on that AIDS vaccine now, huh?

FUN

AT

AIRPORTS

A pilot gets on the loud-speaker shortly after takeoff and says to the passengers, "Folks, welcome aboard flight seven-eighty-nine to Cleveland. We'll be flying at thirty-five thousand feet, and expect to land in an hour and a half. Sit back, relax, and enjoy the flight."

He forgets to turn his microphone off, and turns to his copilot, yawns, and says, "Why don't you take over for a while? I'm going to take me a big healthy shit, and then I'm gonna go fuck the brains out of that pretty blonde flight attendant working back in coach."

His announcement goes over the whole plane. The pretty blonde

flight attendant back in coach hears it and exclaims, "Oh my God!"
and starts running up toward the cockpit.

An old lady sitting in one of the aisle seats stops her and says,
"Relax, honey. He's gotta take a shit first."

I love the electric carts at the airports.

I've become fascinated with them ever since I started flying.
They're always full of old folks and little children, missing business people and vacationers by inches as they snake in and out
of the crowds. Old folks and small children: the royalty of the
modern airport. The rest of us have to walk.

At least the drivers are polite. They always yell "Watch out
for the cart please!" as they pass you, so that you hear the word
"please" as it's spinning you around and knocking over your
luggage.

That would be hard to live down, being hit by one of those
carts. Not being able to dodge an electric airport cart would
be like a running back not being able to out-juke a defensive
lineman.

Sometimes, the carts have canopies on them. You know, because the sun is so bright in the airport. Wouldn't want the old
folks and kids to get a burn, now would we?

On my days off from traveling, I've started to loiter around
Los Angeles airport in my suit, and then when the person in
charge of the carts turns his or her back at the right time . . . I
steal one.

It takes just a second for me to whip off my jacket and tie
and throw on the official-looking red vest I keep in my brief-
case. Then it's off to the races!

"Cart! Excuse the cart please!" I yell. I don't even pick anyone up half the time. I just yell and race around like a maniac.

And boy, you should see people jump. Some of the most-feared corporate executives in the world fly from LAX, and they just freak out and run for their lives when I come barreling through. "Cart! Watch the cart!"

And you know what? Everyone is so used to having maniacs zipping around in electric carts that I've never been caught. I've never even been questioned. I have gotten a few compliments from the airport staff, however. "Way to drive!" or "Jesus, you scared that fat guy!"

If I get tired of the carts, which is rare, I start pushing old people around in their wheelchairs. They're not hard to find (the wheelchairs or the old people), and if you're wearing the red vest, well . . . it's better than a cop uniform as far as gaining someone's trust.

I don't go anyplace special with the old folks, and I never hurt them. I just wheel them around and make siren noises at the top of my lungs. Try it sometime. They love it!

We sing, roll around in patterns, hit some of the business people that I missed in the cart, it's great. Then, after I get tired, I just drop them off at whatever gate is handy. "Looks like you're going to Detroit! Thanks! Gotta go!"

They never complain, and always thank me for being such a nice young man.

Another fun thing I like to do at the airport is dress up in a fake priest outfit and beg for money. (Sometimes, if I'm feeling kinky, I dress as a nurse.)

I got the idea from people that ask for money at LAX, dressed as priests and nurses. They claim they're not, but they have the black collar with the white tab in the middle, and white dresses with that big starched nurse hat, so what would *you* call them? "I'm wearing a big red nose and floppy shoes, but I'm not a clown."

I make up some cause that I work for (fighting drugs and homelessness are best if you want to make the big money. Stay away from orphans and landmark preservation. Nobody cares about that), and then just shake a plastic bucket at innocent travelers who want nothing more than to get to their plane without having a guilt trip laid on them. Just like the real fake priests and nurses do.

And you know what? I make a fortune! Two, three hundred dollars a day sometimes! It's almost as good as when I go to Vegas and play "hooker."

Not that it's the money I care about. I mean, it's nice, but it's not my main motivation.

Like everything else I do at the airport, I do it for the thrill.

LIFE
WITHOUT
FOOTBALL

A guy gets put into a nursing home by his son. He doesn't know if he's going to like it at first, but he decides to give it a shot for his son's sake.

The first morning in the nursing home he wakes up with a hard-on. Out of nowhere, a beautiful nurse walks in, kneels down, and blows him without saying a word.

The guy gets on the phone to his son and says, "Son! I love this place! Thank you so much for putting me in this nursing home!"

The son says, "Wow, Pop. You sound really happy. What happened?"

The old man says, "You won't believe it. I woke up this morning with a hard-on, and the most beautiful nurse I've ever seen in my life came into my room and blew me. Didn't say a word. Just blew me."

"Well, that sounds great, Dad. Congratulations."

"Well, thank you, Son," the old man says, and hangs up the phone.

Later that day, the old man is walking down the hall in his walker. He slips and falls and can't get up. A big hillbilly orderly comes up to him, rips his pants down, fucks him up the ass, and leaves him lying there in a heap.

The old man crawls to a phone and calls his son. "You gotta get me out of here, Son, this place is nuts!"

"What happened, Pop? You sound terrible!" says the son.

"Well, I was walking with my walker and I fell down and couldn't get up. Then this big hillbilly orderly came by, ripped my pants down, and fucked me up the ass!"

"Well you know, Dad," says the son. "You got a blow job this morning. You gotta take the good with the bad . . ."

"No, you don't understand, Son!" exclaims the old man. "I only get a hard-on once a month! I fall down three, four times a day!"

I have the distinct pleasure of owning a home in two major cities in the United States without an NFL franchise. And you know what? I don't care anymore.

I grew up in Cleveland as a die-hard Browns fan. I was one of those guys who would get drunk and cry if they lost a big game, and just get drunk if they lost a small one.

I now live most of the year in Los Angeles, which used to have two NFL teams, the Raiders and the Rams. I didn't care about either one of them, but once in a while the Browns would come to town and I could see them play live, so that was nice.

Now, all three teams play somewhere else and I couldn't give a damn. To hell with all of them.

Art Modell, the owner of the Browns, moved the team to Baltimore because he claimed he was losing money owning the most popular sports franchise in the history of Cleveland. In other words, he's a dumb ass. They now play in Baltimore and have the fear-inspiring name the "Ravens." Even their uniforms are ugly.

I bought a satellite dish and pay extra for the NFL football package just so I can watch them lose, and they hardly ever disappoint me. Show me a good loser, and I'll show you the Baltimore Ravens.

Art Modell suffered a heart attack a few years back while he was still in Cleveland. I hope he has another one. I don't want him to die, I just want him to keep having heart attacks because I know they hurt.

As much as the city of Cleveland was up in arms about the Browns leaving, you barely heard a peep out of the people in Los Angeles when their football teams packed up and went. Especially the Rams. They were such a losing cause anyway. They lost game after game, playing in a stadium that was always half full. Nobody cared if the Rams lived or died. You could drive all over Los Angeles and its surrounding counties and hardly ever see anyone wearing anything with "Rams" written on it. They would be too embarrassed.

The main reason that they moved, though, is that the owner of the Rams is a money-grubbing madwoman who got a zillion dollars to move them. She inherited the team after her husband died, and has the annoying habit that a lot of people have that inherit their money: She acts like she earned it herself. I wouldn't trust her to run a laundromat, let alone a multimillion-dollar sports franchise. Good riddance, and God spare the good people of St. Louis, where she currently makes her vulture's nest.

It was nothing compared to the uproar when the Browns left Cleveland, but a little more was made of it when the Raiders left LA. That's because the logo of the Raiders is so popular with gangs and other juvenile delinquents. Also, they went back to Oakland, where they belonged in the first place, so I think a lot of people were glad to see them back home even if they did miss seeing them play in LA.

The city of Cleveland currently has the name "Cleveland Browns" in a trust, as well as the Browns' colors and records. The NFL has promised us a team by the end of the century. No one knows if the team will come from some other poor city full of suckers who still believe in the tradition of the NFL, or if it will be an expansion franchise. The papers are full of speculation about that, but I don't think that Clevelanders really care, as long as they get a team. Right now, Cleveland is like a single mother who's desperate to find a father for her kids. Anybody decent will do.

I'll believe we're getting a new team when I see it.

In the meantime, I've found plenty to do on Sundays. Who needs the NFL with all of their stupid rules like the "no taunting" rule? No taunting. In the NFL! You can hit a guy at full speed and put him in the hospital, but you can't say "Nah nah! Quarterback has a big butt!" I'd like to meet the sissy that inspired that rule. Probably a kicker.

Who needs game-saving heroics by the home team, and exciting fourth-quarter comebacks led by Bernie Kosar. *The X*

Files is on Sunday! Did you ever see the one where something happened with some aliens? Or the time the government tried to cover something up? And I love how their cell phones work everywhere no matter what.

Okay, so I lied. There really isn't much else for me to do on Sundays except go to the movies or sleep.

A friend of mine suggested I join him in bird watching, but you can forget that. I have to question the sanity of bird watchers. I mean, I thought watching golf was a waste of time, but watching a bird? Maybe if they were having sex, but even then what kind of a life would I have? "Dear Diary, today I watched hummingbirds fuck."

What I end up doing mostly is watching NFL games on my satellite dish and rooting for whoever plays the Ravens. The rest of the games, well, it might as well be hummingbirds going at it for all the interest I have in who wins.

But I still watch. I watch happy fans cheering and excited about what happens to their team and I think, "Just a couple more years, baby."

Go Browns.

LIVE LONG
AND
PROSPER

**A** woman gets a call
from the hospital. The doctor at the hospital says, "Mrs. Smith, it's
about your husband. He's been in a terrible car accident."

Mrs. Smith says, "Ohmigod. What happened?"

The doctor says, "Well, I've got good news, and bad news."

Mrs. Smith says, "Give me the bad news first."

The doctor says, "Well, your husband suffered extensive injuries
and will take years to recuperate. He broke both of his arms, among
other things, so for at least a year you'll have to spoon-feed him, bathe
him, and even wipe his ass for him."

Mrs. Smith says, "My God, that's awful. What's the good news?"
The doctor laughs and says, "I was just teasing you! He's dead!"

They say that exercise and proper diet are the keys to a longer, healthier life.

Oh well.

I know that I make a lot of jokes about it, but I'm not really happy about the way I look lately. I'm fat (220 pounds as of this morning), I'm pale (I never go out), and I'm starting to grow hair on my back. My dream of finally being able to make it with an eighteen-year-old cheerleader is slipping through my fingers.

So, I'm going to lose the weight.

I'm going to lose the weight, get a light tan, and get my back waxed. And, I'm going to buy a cheerleader outfit for the next girl I start dating. A cheerleader outfit and a riding crop. Why hold back?

To everyone reading this, I pledge that I will weigh 180 by the end of this year, or I will donate a huge sum of money to my favorite . . . er . . . I'll . . . I won't buy the cheerleader outfit.

It's going to be tough. I really like eating at Bob's Big Boy, and Denny's. And Cracker Barrel, and Bob Evan's, and Perkin's, and McDonald's, and Burger King, and all the rest of them. Although I will say that Denny's is always my last choice. The only comfort you can take from eating at a Denny's is that you know for sure that all over America, everyone else at a Denny's is just as unhappy as you are.

That's . . . let me see . . . forty pounds in six months. Ouch. That's gonna hurt when I have to cut a leg off in December.

Okay, I won't cut off my leg. I'll just be humiliated by having claimed in public that I would do something and then not follow through with it. I'd rather cut off my leg.

I'm not really doing this for vanity, to be honest, and the cheerleader stuff was just a joke. (The riding crop part wasn't, though.) I'm doing it because I just had a physical, and my cholesterol level is somewhere around the 280s. (I'd look up the exact number but I'm afraid to. I know it's high, and that's good enough for me.) I'm thirty-nine now, and my father had a lot of heart attacks and died when he was forty-five. I don't want to think I only have six years left to live.

I'm doing it because I'd like to live long enough to enjoy my money. Maybe do a couple of movies. Have a kid. I'm doing it because I don't want to die.

Plus, I'm just at the point where if I don't lose weight, I won't be able to buy clothes at a regular store anymore. I have an eighteen-inch neck for crying out loud. The biggest you can find without having the salesman search in the back room is a seventeen and a half. I don't think that people will accuse me of being a sellout for losing weight when all I really want is to be able to buy a shirt that I can button up all the way.

I really think that making my weight-loss plan public will help me do it. I know that a lot of people would like to lose their weight in secret. Quietly and quickly. That's why fad diets always make money.

Fat people don't want strangers laughing at them as they trudge down the street in their sweatpants, or plod clumsily through an aerobics class. They want to take a pill on Friday, walk into work on Monday, and have people go, "Holy cow! What happened to you?! What happened to all that fat?"

And then they would say, "Oh, *that*. It was nothing, really."

Fad diets are dangerous, though. I'm telling you, if you eat enough celery sticks and Dexedrine, somebody's gonna get killed. Either you'll keel over while trying to walk up a flight of stairs, or you'll end up shooting someone just to watch them die.

No, sad to say, the only way to safely lose weight is to eat right and exercise. I might have to (gulp!) join a health club, or start cooking for myself. By cooking, I mean steamed vegetables and rice, things like that. Not ordering a pizza, the way I cook for myself now.

As far as exercising goes . . . watch for my next book, *How I Died While Jogging.*

SINGLE

MAN

BLUES

ow many militant femi-
nists does it take to change a lightbulb?

Two.

One to change the bulb, and one to suck my dick.

That's right. I said suck my dick. 'Cause I've had it. I'm tired
of being pushed around. Tired of being grouped in with all the
dead-beat dads and rapists and lecherous bosses just because I'm

a man. All men aren't "potential rapists." I'm not a potential rapist.

But, I am a potential murderer if all of you don't shut the fuck up and get out of my face already.

You've ruined it for everybody. Everybody, do you hear me? Men, women, everybody. Because of you and everyone else in this society that needs to play political victim and go to court instead of just dealing with it themselves, no one can have any kind of fun anymore. Men and women can't flirt, or hug, or look at anyone sideways because of you and your lawyers. Are you happy? You've used a stink bomb to kill a few ants.

Here's what got me started: At Warner Brothers Studios, where *The Drew Carey Show* is produced, they had several sexual harassment lawsuits pending against various people on the lot last year and it became a worry for management. It's like this all over America, not just Warner Brothers in Burbank. I'm not trying to single them out. Warner Brothers is, in fact, the best place I've ever worked in my life, and I think it's a shame when a great company like this one has to go to these kinds of extreme measures because of the complaints of a few people.

Because of these lawsuits, everyone who works on the Warner Brothers lot, including me, had to attend a sexual harassment seminar this past year, and sign a dated form acknowledging said attendance. Kind of a "cover our ass" program for any future lawsuits that happen because of something that took place on Warner Brothers property. Plus, they don't want to see the stars of their expensive-to-produce television shows and movies being dragged through court on sexual harassment charges, merited or otherwise, because it harms the bottom line value of the shows.

Everybody had to attend. Everybody. Myself, my cast, all the writers. They went all over the lot giving this seminar. Warner Brothers had around twenty-five television shows on the air last year (not to mention movies and everything else they do), more than any other studio, including such popular favorites as *Friends, ER, Murphy Brown, Living Single, The Wayans Brothers, Lois and Clark,* and *Family Matters.* The cast, writers, and producers from all these shows had to take the seminar. So did all their camera crews and prop people and production assistants. It was a real Nazi roundup.

Basically, what the Warner Brothers lawyers said was this: If you hug someone, you can be sued. If you don't hug someone, but just get too much into their "personal space," you can be sued. If ten people laugh at a dirty joke and one doesn't, you can be sued. (They can sue you even if they do laugh, claiming that they were afraid not to laugh at your dirty joke because you were the boss. The joke doesn't even have to be dirty. It just has to be possible for the offended party to construe it as dirty.) If you hang up a cartoon with any perceived sexual content, you can be sued. If you make light of sexual harassment lawsuits, you could be sued (because you would be contributing to an environment where sexual harassment wasn't taken seriously) so don't even joke about it.

So congratulations. You've made my workplace, and from what I understand from the papers, every workplace in America into Salem, Massachusetts.

Especially if you're well-known like I am. I'm like fucking Tituba with a target on my back now that the Warner Brothers lawyers have explained to everyone how they can sue me. I mean, forget it. It doesn't matter if I do anything or not. Just being accused would be enough to hurt my career. Here comes some happy sap with a little bit of money, I look one second too long at your tits and *bam*! I'm in court. What do I have to do now? Carry a video camera on my head to record every-thing I do and say to prove my innocence? Fuck you.

I'm not putting up with it, I tell you. If I like someone, I'm giving them a hug. If I want to tell a joke, I'm telling it. I'm not going to stop being human. And neither should anyone else. You don't like it? Too bad.

If you're offended by dirty jokes and normal flirting, fine. Be offended. Be offended and shut up about it. Go fuck yourself. We shouldn't have to make everything that makes you queasy against company policy.

I'm tired of worrying about accidentally offending someone every time I open my mouth. Or having to look around the room every time I want to tell a joke to see if it's cool.

Besides, if I've just met someone and want to tell an "off-color" joke, I warn them ahead of time anyway. And if they don't want to hear it, I don't tell it; or I tell it at a later time when they're not around. Simple civility should be enough. I don't need to have the threat of legal action hanging over my head for seventy-plus hours a week.

(By the way, if you happen to work for Warner Brothers in Burbank, don't leave this lying around. You could be next.)

And it's not just women, ha ha ha. Men can sue for sexual harassment in the workplace too, and I hope that they work the shit out of this law. In fact, I wish I worked in an office with a woman boss now so I could do just that.

The very first time she ever said, "Hey, nice suit," I'd be calling my lawyer.

"That's right, your honor. She always made it a point to compliment me on my appearance. Yes, she patted my back on several occasions. Unwanted pats." Then, I would break down sobbing and let my female boss pay a big huge settlement. To me. Because she was a woman and I knew I could get away with it.

I know that genuine sexual harassment is wrong. My mother taught me that. I know, I know, I know. I don't need it written down in a company manual. But one uptight person shouldn't be able to stop the whole office from enjoying a dirty joke once in a while. That shouldn't be a sexual harassment issue. And I should be able to let any of the women who work on my show give me a hug if they want to without me freezing up and waiting for a lawyer to jump out of the closet. I mean, it's ridiculous. People have a right to have fun and be relaxed at their workplace.

And while I'm at it . . .

Naval aviators, who are willing to die so that we can have low prices at the gas pump, should be able to throw the wildest parties they can manage without one uptight biddy coming in and stopping it. There were scads of women at that Tailhook party who were having the time of their lives, voluntarily being just as debauched as any of the men. Everyone who flew a plane or even knew someone who flew a plane knew how wild those parties were and what went on. What did she expect? A prayer service? And why didn't she just throw some punches of her own when these couple of guys groped her? Why didn't she give them what they had coming and just kick them in the balls? Didn't our tax money go to teach her how to fight?

I'm not trying to make the idiotic "she had it coming" argument here, which would go something like "of course they grabbed her tits, look how big they are."

Plus, just reaching out and grabbing some tits is wrong no matter what. When I was in college, even at our most drunken fraternity parties we never acted like that. No matter how hard I try I can't think of an excuse good enough to do something like that. But it's still nothing to lose a career over.

Besides, fighter pilots are *supposed* to be aggressive assholes. That's what we pay them for.

I don't know about you, but I don't want a navy full of fighter pilots who've been to a sensitivity seminar. I want mad-dog, rabid killers going to battle for me and mine. Men *and* women. When our stable gas prices are threatened by a Middle-Eastern Madman, when we want to force our form of government on some poor, unsuspecting Latin American country, when uppity foreign diplomats "forget" to pay their parking tickets, I want to be able to call on men and women who like to fight and drink and fuck. I want a naval officer who knows how to whack some drunk in the balls when he grabs her tits, not call a press conference and a lawyer. If you're a wimp who doesn't know how to find the exit at a rowdy party, go fly a kite, not a jet fighter.

101

BIG-DICK

JOKES

t would be redundant to begin
this chapter with a dirty joke.

A few years ago, I was lucky enough to be cast as the third banana
on a short-lived NBC comedy called The Good Life. The star of the
show was one of the nicest, funniest, and hardest-working guys I've
ever known: John Caponera. You can blame him for this chapter.

One of the scenes we did had a megaphone as a prop. During camera
rehearsal, just to get a laugh, John stuck his dick into the small end of
the megaphone. He turned sideways so the cameras couldn't see it, and
yelled, "Hey Drew, check it out!" Then he waggled it at me.

I laughed along with him, and said, "You call that a dick? My dick is so big that . . ." and told a big-dick joke that I'd always wanted to tell but never had the nerve to do on stage. So that day, and for the rest of the time we taped the show, we came in trying to out-do each other coming up with big-dick jokes. He even called me once at two in the morning just to tell me one. I thought of another joke right away, told it to him, and then hung up and went back to sleep.

A few of our other friends started joining in our game, and I began to keep a list in my head. For a while, I considered writing a book under an assumed name and calling it 101 Big-Dick Jokes. *(For the record, my assumed name was going to be Ted Kennedy.) I was going to put one dick joke on each page with an amusing illustration of the joke on the opposite page, and then sell it at truck stops and dirty bookstores. One comic that I worked in a movie with, Taylor Negron, took my* 101 Big-Dick Jokes *idea seriously and wanted to write it with me. We were going to go to Vegas to write it in a weekend, sitting around the pool at Caesar's in a drunken stupor and thinking them up. I don't know which ones of these are his, but two or three of them are, and I'd like to thank him for letting me use them.*

Although the majority of these were written by me, I have to be fair and tell you that there are some of them that were thought up by friends of mine over the years when my "big-dick joke" idea came up in conversation. I'll give them credit for the jokes I'm sure that they thought up.

None of the men involved with this chapter have big dicks, that I know of. Neither do I. Not that it's small, it's just not big enough to make a joke about.

1. My dick is so big, there's still snow on it in the summertime. *(John Caponera)*

2. My dick is so big, I went to The Viper Room and my dick got right in. I had to stand there and argue with the doorman.

3. My dick is so big, I have to call it Mr. Dick in front of company.

4. My dick is so big, it won't return Spielberg's calls. *(Terry Mulroy)*

5. My dick is so big, it graduated a year ahead of me from high school.

6. My dick has an elevator and a lobby.

7. My dick has better credit than I do.

8. My dick is so big, clowns climb out of it when I cum.

9. My dick is so big, it was once overthrown by a military coup. It's now known as the Democratic Republic of My Dick.

10. My dick is so big, it has casters. *(Les Firestein)*

11. My dick is so big, I'm already fucking a girl tomorrow.

12. My dick is so big, ships use it to find their way into the harbor. *(Caponera)*

13. My dick is so big, there was once a movie called *Godzilla vs. My Dick.*

14. My dick is so big, it lives next door.

15. My dick is so big, I entered it in a big-dick contest and it came in first, second, and third.

16. My dick is so big, it votes.

17. My dick is a better dresser than I am.

18. My dick is so big, it has a three-picture deal.

19. My dick is so big that the head of it has only seen my balls in pictures. *(Eddie Gorodetsky)*

20. My dick is so big, Henry Aaron used it to hit his 750th home run.

21. My dick runs the 440 in fifteen seconds.

22. My dick is the Walrus, koo koo ga joob. *(Mulroy)*

23. No matter where I go, my dick always gets there first.

24. My dick takes longer lunches than I do.

25. My dick contributed $50,000 to the Democratic National Committee.

26. My dick was once the ambassador to China.

27. My dick is so big, it's gone condo. *(Jason Stuart)*

28. My dick hit .370 in the minors before it hurt its knee.

29. My dick was almost drafted by the Cleveland Browns, but Art Modell didn't want a bigger dick than he was on the team.

30. My dick is so big, I use the Eiffel Tower as a French tickler. *(Carey and Firestein)*

31. It's so big, when it rains the head of my dick doesn't get wet.

32. My dick is so big, I could wear it as a tie if I wasn't so afraid of getting a hard-on and killing myself.

33. My dick is so big, I have to use an elastic zipper.

34. My dick is so big, it has feet.

35. My dick is so big, a homeless family lives underneath it. *(Firestein)*

36. My dick is so big, it takes four fat women and a team of Clydesdales to jack me off.

37. My dick is so big, my mother was in labor for three extra days.

38. My dick is so big, they use the bullet train to test my condoms. *(Marcy Woolard)*

39. My dick is so big, it has investors. *(Firestein)*

40. My dick is so big, it seats six.

41. My dick is so big, I use a hula hoop as a cock ring. *(Firestein)*

42. My dick is so big, we use it at parties as a limbo pole. *(Ginger M.)*

43. My dick is so big, King Kong is going to crawl up it in the next remake. *(Firestein)*

44. My dick is so big, it has an opening act.

45. My dick is so big I can fuck an elevator shaft.

46. My dick is so big, it has its own Wheaties box. *(Firestein)*

47. My dick is so big, I have to cook it breakfast in the mornings.

48. My dick is so big, the city had to carve a hole in the middle of it so cars could get through.

49. My dick is so big, every time I get hard I cause a solar eclipse.

50. My dick is so big, it only plays arenas. *(Rick Messina, who isn't kidding)*

51. If you cut my dick in two, you can tell how old I am.

52. My dick was once set on fire for a Dino DiLaurentis movie.

53. My dick is so big, it needs an airplane warning light. *(Firestein)*

54. My dick is so big, Trump owns it.

55. My dick is so big, that we're all a part of it, and it's all a part of us. *(Mulroy)*

56. My dick is so big, I can never sit in the front row.

57. My dick is so big, it has its own dick. And even my dick's dick is bigger than your dick.

58. My dick is so big, you can't blow me without a ladder.

59. My dick is so big, it only does one show a night.

60. My dick is so big, you can ski down it.

61. My dick is so big, it has an elbow.

62. My dick is so big, I have to check it as luggage when I fly.

63. My dick is so big, it has a personal trainer.

64. My dick is so big, that right now it's in the other room fixing us drinks.

65. My dick is so big, it has a retractable dome.

66. My dick is so big, it has stairs up the center like the Statue of Liberty.

67. My dick is so big there's a sneaker named "Air My Dick." *(Firestein)*

68. My dick is so big, I'm its bitch. *(Firestein)*

69. My dick is so big, it's against the law to fuck me without protective headgear.

70. My dick is so big, I could fuck a tuba.

71. My dick is so big, Stephen Hawking has a theory about it. *(Gorodetsky)*

72. My dick is so big, it has its own gravity.

73. NASA once launched a space probe to search for the tip of my dick.

74. My dick is so big, it's impossible to see all of it without a satellite.

75. The inside of my dick contains billions and billions of stars.

76. My dick is so big, it has a spine.

77. My dick is so big, it has a basement.

78. My dick is so big, movie theatres now serve popcorn in small, medium, large, and My Dick. *(Gorodetsky)*

79. My dick is more muscular than I am.

80. My dick is so big it has cable.

81. My dick is so big, it violates seventeen zoning laws.

82. My dick is so big, it has its own page in the Sierra Club calendar. *(Firestein)*

83. My dick is so big, it has a fifty-yard line.

84. My dick is so big, I was once in Ohio and got a blow job in Tennessee. *(Monty Hoffman)*

85. My dick is so big, Las Vegas casinos fly it into town for free.

86. My dick is so big, I can braid it.

87. My dick is so big, that when it's Eastern Standard Time at the tip, it's Central Mountain Time at my balls. *(Gorodetsky)*

88. My dick is so big, I painted the foreskin red, white, and blue and used it as a flag.

89. My dick is so big, I can sit on it.

90. My dick is so big, it can chew gum.

91. My dick is so big, it only tips with hundreds.

92. My dick is so big, the Carnegie Deli named a sandwich after it. *(Carey)*

   Actually, two sandwiches. *(Firestein)*

93. My dick is so big, the city was going to build a statue of it but they ran out of cement.

94. My dick is so big, Michael Jackson wants to build an amusement park on it.

95. My dick is so big, when I get hard my eyebrows get pulled down to my neck.

96. My dick is so big, you're standing on it.

97. My dick is so big, it only comes into work when it feels like it.

98. My dick is so big, it plays golf with the president.

99. My dick is so big, it charges money for its autograph.

100. My dick is so big, it has an agent. My dick's people will call your people. Let's have lunch with my dick.

101. My dick is so big, it's right behind you.

BEER

WHAT'S MIMI REALLY LIKE?

There's a pair of Siamese twin sisters, joined at the hip. One plays the saxophone, and the other one is a nymphomaniac. They're both big Julio Iglesias fans.

One day, they notice that Julio Iglesias is going to perform in their town, so they decide to go.

While they're sitting there in the front row, the nymphomaniac Siamese twin starts making eyes at Julio. He notices and starts making eyes back at her. This goes on for the whole show, and the twins end up getting invited backstage to his dressing room where Julio and the nymphomaniac Siamese twin go at it with each other all around the *room. They do it in every conceivable position, while the other Siamese twin hangs on for dear life and plays romantic music on her saxophone for them.*

A year goes by, and the Siamese twins notice that Julio Iglesias is going to be performing in their town again.

"Hey," the nymphomaniac Siamese twin says, "Julio Iglesias is coming back to town! Maybe we should call him up so we can get together with him again and party."

"Oh, forget it," says the other one. "He'll never remember us."

What's Mimi really like?

That's the question I get asked the most, right after "Where's Mimi?" and "When are you and Mimi going to get together?" The answers to which are "I don't know," and "Never."

Kathy Kinney, the actress who plays Mimi, is the total opposite of the character she plays on TV. She's one of the nicest people I've ever met, never raising her voice or showing any signs of bad temper. Ever.

She rarely wears makeup, and if she does, she wears very little. Also, she never dresses in any wild clothes.

She's a total professional, never blowing a line or failing to deliver a joke.

She's lots of fun, everyone loves her, and we're lucky to have her on the show.

There. That's what Mimi is really like.

Now shut the hell up about it.

THE CRITICS SPEAK!

A drunk walks into a bar and says to the bartender, *"Hey, if I show you a trick will you give me a free drink?"*

The bartender says, "I don't know. Show me the trick first and we'll see."

The drunk pulls a frog out of his pocket and sets him down at the piano where the frog proceeds to play the best jazz the bartender's ever heard. Amazed, the bartender gives the drunk his free drink.

Then the drunk says, "Hey bartender, if I show you another trick, can I get another free drink?"

The bartender says, "If it's anything like the trick you just showed me you can drink the rest of the night for free."

So the drunk pulls a rat from his other pocket, puts it on top of the piano, and the rat starts singing scat along with the frog's jazz riffs. The bartender starts pouring drinks for the drunk as fast as he can drink them.

A few hours later, an agent walks into the bar and sees the frog and the rat going at it on the piano. He says to the bartender, "Why, that's the greatest act I've ever seen! Who owns that act?"

The bartender points to the drunk, who's passed out on the floor and says, "That drunk owns them."

The agent wakes the drunk up and says, "That's the greatest act I've ever seen in my life. I'll give you a hundred thousand dollars for that act."

The drunk says, "They're not for sale."

The agent says, "Okay then, I'll give you fifty thousand just for the scat-singing rat."

The drunk says, "Okay, it's a deal," and the agent gives him the fifty thousand and leaves with the rat.

The bartender yells at the drunk, "I can't believe you just did that! You had a million dollar act there, and you just broke it up for a measly fifty grand!"

"Relax," the drunk says. "The frog's a ventriloquist."

What I've done in this chapter is put together some of the worst reviews *The Drew Carey Show* got when it first premiered. Plus, I threw in a couple of angry letters from viewers, who are the most vicious critics of all.

I'm doing this just for fun. Now that it's considered a "hit show," I think it's an interesting exercise to go back and see what people thought of it when it first came out. None of these criticisms ever got me angry or sad, or even affected the outcome of the show. They're just opinions of good people who had only the pilot of the show to go by. And admittedly, the show has gotten a lot better since then, so maybe they had a point. Besides, most of the reviews we got were great, which made the negative ones easy to ignore.

The only thing that ever really got me going back when *The Drew Carey Show* premiered was when they would compare my show to *Friends*. In the fall of '95, critics compared every show that didn't have a child in it to *Friends*. That year, they were right about that more than they were wrong, but they were wrong about my show and it used to burn me up.

A lot of people think that this means I don't like *Friends*, and that couldn't be further from the truth. It's a great show. It's funny, well-written, and well-acted. The cast members from *Friends* that I have met on the Warner Brothers lot have all been very nice to me. Of course, like everyone else, I got tired of seeing them on the cover of *every* magazine at the newsstand like they were the Second Coming, but that wasn't their fault and I don't hold it against them. (And I hope it never happens to me. What a curse, having every magazine cover screaming how good-looking and funny and perfect you are. I would throw myself off a bridge.)

Now, normally, a guy wouldn't bitch about having his show compared to a super-popular mega-hit, except that they compared us to the wrong show. We thought that our show was closer in tone to *Roseanne,* or *Grace Under Fire.* And, it was about a lone, overweight office worker in his thirties. It's not about a *group* of people, it's about one guy. It's set in the Midwest. *Gilligan's Island* was more like *Friends* than we were. (More than one main character, living way better than they could afford to in real life, one character having a crush on the other, at least two characters you dreamed of having sex with, a monkey. . . .)

Because of the comparisons, I was afraid the audience that we needed to like us wouldn't even tune in to begin with, and then I'd be off the air. I knew that the first few weeks usually makes or breaks you, and being lumped in with a group of shows that *were* like *Friends* and had nothing to do with ours in either tone or content aggravated me to no end. We worked so hard to *not* be like those other shows, and every time I read that we were just like *Friends*, I saw our whole potential fan base missing us and my whole career going down the drain.

And, by saying we were a "*Friends* clone" they implied that we ripped *Friends* off somehow, that we stole the idea of having six impossibly attractive single people trading wisecracks in an apartment complex in New York which none of them could really afford to live in. The headlines would always be something like "Make Way for the *Friends* Clones," or "It's a Fall Full of *Friends* Rip-offs." Then, there would be my picture with everyone else's. For a while there, all someone had to do was whisper "Friends" in my ear and I would go punch a wall. And everytime I heard "I'll Be There for You" on the radio, I'd want to drive my car off the road. (I like the song now, though.)

To make matters worse, *Friends* is produced by Warner Brothers, so we film our shows on the same lot. And of course, they make the most money, they get the highest ratings, they're really nice people, they're all good-looking, blah blah blah. Or if it's not them, it's *ER* (another one of my favorite shows), also filmed at Warner Brothers. It's like living in the same house with a perfect older brother and sister when you're the family screw-up. But, on the bright side, it keeps you from getting a big head.

This past spring was the best example. Besides *ER* and *Friends,* they were filming the third *Batman* movie on the Warner Brothers lot, too. Let me tell you something: When you have extremely popular, well-liked money makers like *Batman, ER,* and *Friends* filming all around you, you pretty much realize that you're not such hot stuff after all, and that you better just shut up and go to work.

Now, other than that *Friends* business, I really like the critics. I meet most of the television critics every year at parties thrown for them by ABC. All the major networks spend thousands of dollars on parties for the TV critics hoping to influence their opinions of the new fall shows. Except for the WB. I think the WB just sends them cash directly.

Almost every critic I've met at these get-togethers, and done interviews with over the course of my run on ABC, has been just the type of person I would like to have as a friend. Intelligent, hard-working, and unafraid to state an opinion. I love people like that.

And boy can they drink. You've never seen such a group of canapé-grabbing booze hounds. If it's free, they'll eat it and drink it. I'm telling you, they're my kind of people. And they're all good-looking. Did I mention that?

So, believe me when I say that I'm not doing this out of any sense of animosity or revenge. I'm just doing this for fun. I'm not doing this so that my fans can look at this and say, "Boy was that person stupid." So please don't write them any letters or make any snide remarks to them if you run into them on the street. I need them to keep liking me or I'll lose my job.

Here's what Ken Tucker (a guy who I really like, honest) from *Entertainment Weekly* said about *The Drew Carey Show* in the September 15, 1995 "Fall TV Preview" issue:

Let's do *Friends*, but with less attractive people!

Ouch. A double whammy.

Hammocked between *Ellen* and *Grace Under Fire*, this has a shot at popularity, but Carey is a much more wooden comic-turned-actor than DeGeneres or Butler.

Oh, man . . . I'm ugly and I can't act. And neither can Ellen or Brett, evidently.

Ken Tucker gave the show a B+ in his review in the May 24, 1996 issue of the magazine, and the whole cast was on the cover of *Entertainment Weekly* in the June 6, 1997 issue ("TV's Winners and Losers"). We were one of the winners.

The Hollywood Reporter actually gave my show a great review when it premiered, but in their September 11, 1995 issue, they let some ad agency swamis try to predict which of the new shows would be hits and which ones wouldn't. They were Betsy Frank of Zenith Media, and Paul Schulman, president of the Paul Schulman Company.

I've since met them both, briefly, on separate occasions in New York City when ABC announced their fall schedules. I got to shake their hands and say hello after they stood in line to get their picture taken with me. They both seem like nice people. Here's what they said in 1995:

The prognosticators were not big fans of ABC's *The Drew Carey Show*. Frank says its star "seemed unable to provide an anchor or a central theme to keep viewers coming back." Schulman also gave "Drew Carey" a thumbs down. "He's not an acceptable lead," Schulman says. "He will not carry that show."

Not an "acceptable lead"? What, just because I'm ugly and I'm a wooden actor I'm unacceptable? I'd like to hear him say that to the great Ronald Reagan.

Paul Schulman, in an interview for the *USA Today*, also said something like "They'd be better off getting Jim Carrey than Drew Carey for the role."

Yeah, well no kidding. I'd rather watch Jim Carrey than Drew Carey, too. Good luck getting him to work for the kind of money I make, though.

They didn't dislike all the shows, though. Betsy Frank said about *Bless This House*: "Not since *Roseanne* has a blue-collar sitcom arrived on the scene with so much heart, soul, and truth." (She's right, it *was* good.)

It was also canceled after CBS put it opposite the show with the star that couldn't provide an anchor or a central theme. You know, the wooden ugly guy who's unacceptable.

Hey! Here's something a pearl of wisdom from my pals at *TV Guide*. Now, I know that the editors of *TV Guide* like the show because they told me so to my face at an expensive dinner that they paid for. You can't get any more sincere than that in Hollywood. But, here's what one of their writers said in the September 16, 1995 Fall Preview issue.

> Maybe you have to live in Cleveland to understand this one. The jokes in the pilot were flat, and despite obvious attempts at wackiness, the writing was mostly formulaic.

Formulaic? That must have been Bruce Helford's half of the script. The half I wrote was brilliant.

Here's what killed me most at the time about that review: Underneath, filling up half a page, is me and the rest of the cast smiling like idiots, in a picture that was taken by . . . *TV Guide!* "Hey, can we take a picture of you guys for our dart board?" "Well, sure! How would you like us to pose?"

But then, in the May 11, 1996 issue, we made *TV Guide*'s "Bring Back These Shows" page.

> Cleveland's crew-cut Carey is a refreshing middle-American alternative to TV's fixation on big-city types. Insecure but philosophically funny, Everyman Drew carries the show . . .

. Ha! You hear that Schulman? "Carries the show!" From the most knowledgeable source of information in the TV business, the magazine that America trusts for the straight scoop on all things television, *TV Guide*. ABC would still be better off with Jim Carrey, but at least I got you on the "carries the show" point.

Now, if I could just find a review that says that I'm "an acceptable lead." Hmmm . . . what's this in this old trunk? Well, lookie here. A copy of the September 18, 1995 issue of *Newsweek*. Oh cool! There's a picture of me right by the headline "So Much TV, So Little Time." *And* I'm the only picture on the page! Wow, I even have my own little sidebar. Man, I can't believe a big, important news weekly is featuring *me* in one of their articles! Wait, there's something written underneath my picture. Let's see what it says:

> *The Drew Carey Show:* An abrasively chipper stand-up comic, Carey is the season's most annoying new star. He plays a self-styled "regular guy" who lives in Cleveland, drinks a lot of beer, and laughs at his own jokes. Somebody has to.

Ow. My ass.

I think about that paragraph every time I get these sneaky, government-looking envelopes from *Newsweek* trying to get me to become a subscriber.

★　★　★

There's more bad reviews, but none as funny or interesting. Mostly stuff like ". . . uninspired and . . . unfocused" (the *Chicago Tribune*, August 27, 1995). To get the really nasty stuff, we have to leave the arena of the professional critic, and go to the people that really count: the American Public. Here's two of them that stand out, and are printable. They also concern the same episode of the show.

It was a show where my character fired a guy named Earl (played by David Cross of HBO's *Mr. Show*) who couldn't do his job anymore because of his mental state. The character then tried to shoot me in my backyard. Also in the show, Mimi found out that she was Polish royalty when a not-too-smart guy from Akron, claiming to be the king of Poland (played by Dan Castellaneta from *The Simpsons*) came up to Cleveland to claim her.

The first letter is from a Ph.D. in Massachusetts, the state that never has failed to elect a Kennedy, no matter how many women they kill or rape, or how drunk they get:

> This program was a disservice to the mentally ill . . . the least you can do is to put pressure on the producers of this abomination to make amends by issuing an apology to one or more of the advocacy groups for the mentally ill (see enclosed list) . . .

Yeah, like I'm going to take the time to write everyone who might be offended by one of our jokes. I'd be doing nothing but writing apologies all day. When I first read her letter, I thought, "What is she, nuts?" without even thinking about it.

The second is from a guy in Minnesota, who claims to be of Polish ancestry:

> Your March 19 show portraying "the king and queen of Po-
> land" was incredibly offensive, not only to 10 million Polish
> Americans, but also to all viewers who are sick and tired of
> the bigotry, dullness, and blithering idiocy that seem to mas-
> querade as "humor" on your show.
>
> Polish Americans will remember this. We will remember
> all bigots and racists like you.

Notice that the mental health lady didn't seem to mind the
Polish jokes, and the Polish guy didn't seem to mind the jokes
about the crazy killer.

Maybe next season we can feature a mentally deranged Polack, so they can get together and form a coalition.

And finally, my favorite letter of all time, published in the *Cleveland Plain Dealer* this year after we did a special show featuring
Mayor of Cleveland Michael White (don't worry, the city
didn't pay for his ticket, we did), ex-Browns quarterback Bernie Kosar, Joe Walsh (who used to live in Cleveland), and Little
Richard (who has family in Cleveland). The show got a lot of
press in Cleveland, to say the least, and so a lot of people there
tuned in who hadn't seen the show before, earning a 48 share
locally. (For those of you unfamiliar with the lingo, a 48 share
means that 48 percent of the people watching TV in Cleveland
that night were watching the show.) This letter was thought-
fully sent to me by one of my relatives.

> We had never watched *The Drew Carey Show* until last night
> (Jan. 29). After being touted by the media about our Mayor
> White and Bernie Kosar making an appearance on his show,
> we decided to watch and see what they could do for the
> image of Cleveland. Well, after a half-hour of sexual innuen-
> does, sleaze, and profane language, our mayor and ex-

quarterback have stooped just about as low as they can get. We perceived them with morals much higher than that. I sure hope the mayor did not use our tax money for this trip out West. I'm glad we have an "off" button to use between eight and ten every evening. Please, Mr. Carey, if all your shows are like that, align yourself with another city.

I'M FROM CLEVELAND! I'M FROM CLEVELAND! I'M FROM CLEVELAND! I'M FROM CLEVELAND! I'M FROM CLEVELAND! I'M FROM CLEVELAND! I'M FROM CLEVELAND!

THE DEPARTMENT OF BROADCAST STANDARDS AND PRACTICES

A man walks into a bank, walks up to one of the women tellers and says, "I want to open a fucking checking account."

She says, "Sir, would you please watch your language!"

He says, "Fuck my language. I want to open a fucking checking account."

She says, "Sir! If you don't watch your language, I'm going to have to get the manager."

He says, "I don't give a damn about watching my fucking language! I want to open a fucking checking account!"

She leaves and gets the manager. The manager walks up to the man and says, "What seems to be the problem?"

He says, "I just won thirty million dollars in the motherfucking lottery, and I want to open a fucking checking account."

The manager jerks his thumb toward the teller and says, "Is this bitch giving you trouble?"

In this chapter, I salute Neil Conrad, the Broadcast Standards and Practices executive from ABC who is assigned to *The Drew Carey Show*. Neil is a fellow Clevelander who's earnest, hard-working, and once you get past the idea that he lives in a democracy and censors people for a living, a hell of a nice guy.

One of the reasons that I like him so much is that he takes his job seriously, but he's not some insane moral crusader. His bosses from ABC in New York tell him the rules, and he tries to enforce them. Joe Censor, earnin' a paycheck.

I wish we could all live without them, and be our own censors, but we're all too weak and easily led, I guess. We need someone to protect us. At least that's the message I get every time I read about the FCC wanting to fine Howard Stern and tell us what words we're not allowed to hear on the radio. That's the message I get every time someone from Congress starts giving out these fascist-type warnings about television "cleaning up its act" before "we clean it up for you."

(That's one of the reasons that every broadcast network has a Standards and Practices Department, you know. To keep the government off their backs. There's a lot of other reasons they have them; advertisers, local affiliates . . . but I think that the biggest reason is to blunt government interference into their business.)

And you know, the government may be right. I mean, I

don't know about you, but if I ever heard the word "fuck" on free broadcast television, I just might lose my will to live. Those "seven words you can't say on television" might give me cancer or put out one of my eyes. I might commit murder if I hear that kind of language on a broadcast network. Of course, I can hear it on cable and in real life, and even read it in a book (sorry). But on regular TV? Anarchy!

Why, poor people might hear that stuff! Then what?

By the way, isn't it great that if you really want to hear "naughty" words and dangerous ideas about sex you have to pay for the privilege? What you can easily buy if you have the money, the government won't let you hear for free. And the harder they try to ban it, the more people seem to want it. (P.S., don't legalize drugs.)

You can't hear the bad words in a song on the radio, where it's free, you have to buy the CD to hear them.

You can't see two adults enjoy sex on free broadcast television. You have to pay for cable, and then, usually, pay extra for the Playboy Channel. (Or rent a porno.)

Being poor sucks that way, huh? The government will let you say "fuck" all you want, but it won't ever let you hear it or see it being done unless you give up some rent money.

Here's another example: Remember the panic about *Ellen* announcing that she was gay? So many people wanted to keep that from happening only because it was on *free TV*. Lesbians, and the idea that homosexuality can be a healthy lifestyle, have been all over cable for years—*if you could afford cable*. In fact, that same night, you could've walked into just about any independent video store and bought yourself a lesbian porno featuring sex acts that *Ellen* didn't even hint at, *if you had already spent big money on a VCR and could afford to purchase or rent the tape*. Which is exactly what I did.

In support of Ellen's coming out, I enjoyed a brilliantly filmed lesbian epic *(Strap-On Sally #3)* on my very own expensive VCR as soon as the *Ellen* show was over. No need to thank me, Ellen. I was glad to do it.

And to all you people who can't afford VCRs or cable TV, don't worry. The government is looking out for you.

Anyway, I don't know why I'm complaining. You can complain all you want and it won't do any good. The Department of Broadcast Standards and Practices will always be there, no matter what. So will the FCC and a meddling politician. You might as well complain about the weather.

Neil's notes to us are usually about offensive language, descriptions of sexual activity or drug use, and warnings not to offend specific, protected ethnic groups—you know, the usual. The memos that he sends us are from the early scripts for each show, and what he sees in rehearsals.

For example, in the script for the pilot for *The Drew Carey Show,* he wanted us to get rid of: two *hells,* two *damns,* one *bastard,* two *sonuvabitches,* one *ass,* the word *pisses,* the mention of Jack Daniel's, and a line which implied that Lewis could purchase and use drugs.

All of his notes come several times a week on a very official-looking, don't-argue-with-us form, and they are broken down by page number.

At the time, I didn't know that Neil looked at the scripts that closely, and I remember being surprised at the first memo. I've since learned how detail-oriented he is.

Here's a note from a memo dated August 8, 1995.

> **Please note the excessive use of hell and damn found on pages 4, 20, 21, 22, 28, 38, 40, and 52, and reduce this number by half.**

But by the following year, he was being a lot nicer about his requests. This one is from August 12, 1996:

> Please note this review is in addition to the previous reviews dated August 7th and 9th. As discussed, please review the uses of "hell" and "damn" found on pages 16, 31, 39, 40, and kindly reconsider the creative necessity of each.

"Well," you may ask, "of course he's going to watch out for foul language; don't you and your writers have anything better to do than to try and slip dirty words past the censor each week?"

The truth is, unfortunately, no, we don't. In fact, October 12, 1995 was one of the darkest days in the history of *The Drew Carey Show.* That's the day when the following memo arrived from Neil's desk:

> Approved as submitted.

Some of the writers were so upset that they had to be sent home. Bruce couldn't eat. I stood near the back entrance of the stage and shook my fist at the sky shouting, "Never again!"

These next notes concern a show where Mr. Bell (my boss during the first year of the show) wanted to replace Mimi (his assistant) with a woman he was having sex with. The script was full of sexual comments:

> Page 2—Lisa's line, "Stop, you're getting me all wet," will not be acceptable.

> Page 10—Suzie's sexual relationship with Mr. Bell has been established, therefore, her reference to "rug burns" will not be acceptable. Mimi's line, "Should I bring a sponge?" must also be deleted.

Page 11—Please delete Drew's line, ". . . there's a condom sticking out of your shoe."

Page 17—The established sexual relationship between Suzie and Mr. Bell makes Drew's reference to her as a "chew toy" unacceptable.

Page 18—Lewis's lines, "Hey, I think I saw this on The Nature Channel. Are you 'presenting rearly'?" will not be acceptable (i.e., delivered while Jay is down on his hands and knees).

Page 23—Please delete Mimi's line, "Especially if he puckers his lips."

Page 52—Mimi's line, "Face up?" will not be acceptable (i.e., referring to a sexual position).

Here's a note that we get all the time:

Page 21—The American Humane Association will be notified of this animal action.

Oh. Well, in that case, we'll leave the puppy alone.

Actually, I can't remember what we were doing with an animal in that episode and I'm too lazy to look it up. I doubt if it was anything bad.

You see, it's the policy of ABC, Warner Brothers, and everybody else to notify the American Humane Association whenever an animal is being used on the set. Then, someone from some animal group (I think it's the same Humane Association) has to be present when the animal is "acting" to make sure that it isn't harmed. Of course, no one cares what happens to the production assistants or the extras, but at least you know the dogs aren't being mistreated.

I love the notes from Neil about sexual things, because he's not allowed to be graphic himself, and it forces him to say things like this:

> Page 38—Please use caution here and on page 39 when Mr. Bell's POV [point of view] goes to Kate's chest. Kate's wardrobe must be suitable for broadcast and free of any nipple impression.

This note was for a sequence in which Mr. Bell was trying to get Kate to go to bed with him. We never saw Mr. Bell in the show (we only heard his voice) and so we came up with an idea to have the camera be his eyes roaming all over Kate's body while she tried to talk business with him. No matter how hard I tried when I watched the final footage we shot, I couldn't see any nip.

And how about you? Is your wardrobe "suitable for broadcast"? Hmmmm? Is it free of any nipple impression?

Here's the other note from that scene:

> Page 39—Again, please exercise good taste when Mr. Bell focuses on Kate's posterior.

Uh . . . gotcha, chief. Will do. (Snicker. Wink. Nudge.)

Here's a favorite of most of the writers. It's from the first show of the '96–'97 season, which had a scene where my new pants tented up every time I sat down, so it looked like I had a huge hard-on.

> Page 19—Here and throughout, the appearance of Drew's pants must clearly be puffy and not pointed.

This next one is my favorite. It was about a courtroom scene in which Mimi was testifying against me and calls me a "butt wipe."

> **Page 24—Please substitute for "butt wipe" in Mimi's line.**

We argued and argued, but Neil wouldn't give in. Finally, we had Mimi call me a "butt weasel" and it was approved.

I personally think that "butt weasel" is much more offensive. I mean, when it comes to your butt, wouldn't you rather have a wipe than a weasel?

There's lots of notes like that from ABC, via Neil, that come down to semantics. Here are some of the more notable ones, with the date of the memo provided in parentheses:

> (Sept. 14, 1995)
> Page 8—The blood effects must not be overdone. Acceptability of the "geyser of blood" will be determined at the time the scene is shot.

> (Oct. 19th, 1995)
> Page 7—Here and again on page 10, "Farty" will not be acceptable as a first name for Wilson.

> (Nov. 2, 1995)
> Page 28—Please substitute "down your throat" for "up your butt" in Mimi's line.

> (Nov. 10, 1995)
> Page 11—As discussed, in order to avoid a display of alcohol abuse or overconsumption please modify Drew's line, "Four drinks," to "One drink."

> (Nov. 16, 1995)
> Page 2—Please substitute "nose" or "ear" for "butt" in Mimi's line.

One of our more famous episodes of the '96–'97 season involved Kate putting fart noises into a training video that I made for work. It's an old gag, and a lot of people have done it, but nobody's ever gotten away with it on network television before.

It was a big argument to get it on the air at all. And not just with Neil. It went all the way up to Neil's bosses and their bosses, and the people above that. I think it finally may have been discussed with God. I know it sounds crazy, but fart noises are a big taboo on network television. Especially if you're talking about probably a hundred fart noises, like we had. (Funny, since most people watching TV are doing exactly that: sitting around, farting.) Back in the seventies, ABC aired the Mel Brooks comedy, *Blazing Saddles*, and wouldn't air the fart noises from the campfire scene, one of the funniest sequences in the movie. Their policy still hadn't changed.

Most of the best arguments about it took place on the phone and on the floor of the stage. I remember Bruce arguing on the phone in the writer's room with a network executive who thought that some of the fart noises sounded "too juicy" and wanted them toned down. Eventually, we kept all the fart noises that we wanted.

Here's Neil's official warning about the SFX (sound effects) in that script:

> Page 37—Here and throughout, the SFX should be a funny, exaggerated, whoopee cushion sound.

They ended up being the grossest fart noises that I've ever heard.

A lot of notes from Neil involve actual, specific people that we might offend in the script, as opposed to just people in general:

(Sept. 20, 1995)
Page 13—The use of "Polack" in any of Drew's dialogue
will not be acceptable.

(Nov. 2, 1995)
Page 8—Please substitute "little person" for "dwarf" in
Drew's line.

(Nov. 3, 1995)
Page 8—Please substitute "little person for "dwarf" in
Drew's line.
(Oops. I guess he does notice if we just ignore him.)

(Dec. 8, 1995)
Page 38—Please ensure Chuck's dialogue concerning stalk-
ing case statistics is accurate or modify his speech.

(Dec. 15, 1995)
Page 27—Pastor Lindemann's line, "One, two, three,
swing!" makes fun of the blind and is unacceptable.

Page 38—Again, the pastor's line derives humor from the
blind. "I'm thinking of having a partially sighted girl bat
clean-up" will not be acceptable.

(Feb. 1, 1996)
Page 2—Please substitute for "spastic" in Chuck's line.

Page 20—Here and on page 22 "Nancy Boy" will not be
acceptable.

(Feb. 2, 1996)
Page 2—Chuck's use of "spastic" continues to be unacceptable.

(Feb. 16, 1996)
Page 41—Please delete Drew's lines, "I'm tired of you of-

fering cigarettes to our nation's youth," and "Maybe it's not so bad that kids smoke" on the following page.

(Sept. 23, 1996)
Page 16—Drew's dialogue concerning *Reader's Digest* should be modified as the cost of the subscription is much less than ninety-five cents a day.

Page 19—As discussed, "seizure" remains unacceptable as a joke in Lewis's line.

(Nov. 11, 1996)
Page 4—Jim's line, ". . . they pay us under the table" referring to Saks, will not be acceptable.

I love this next bunch of notes because when they're taken out of context like they are here, it sounds like we were out to destroy the entire moral fabric of the United States. We weren't, of course. And even if we were, Neil wouldn't let us.

(Sept. 14, 1995)
Page 3—Please delete Woman #3's line, ". . . and use his cajones as a carrying handle."

(Nov. 10, 1995)
Page 39—Jay's line, "And Kate, unclench your sphincter, . . ." will not be acceptable.

(Feb. 9, 1996)
Page 32—Kate's line ". . . and my mom's been hitting her old bong again" will not be acceptable.

(Oct. 9, 1996)
Please substitute for "human skin" in Drew's line.

(Oct. 17, 1996)
Page 11—Kate's line ". . . grab your ankles, we're gonna doggy dance" is too graphic and will not be acceptable.

(Oct. 21, 1996)
Page 12—Kate's line, "Grab your socks, we're gonna doggy dance" remains unnacceptable.

(Oct. 31, 1996)
Page 22—Here and throughout, please delete any reference to a "Legalize Marijuana Float."

(Nov. 4, 1996)
Page 23—Drew's line "Also, I'm not sayin' I approve of the 'Legalize Marijuana Float . . .' " remains unacceptable for broadcast.

(Nov. 8, 1996. From a show were we portrayed Santa Claus as a child-hating drunk and had him die of a heart attack in front of the kids.)
Page 27—The dialogue exchange beginning with Oswald's line, "Five bucks to whoever can cut the cheese on Santa" through Lewis's line, "I've got proof here that Santa's a bastard" will not be acceptable. The action of Santa grabbing his crotch will also be unacceptable.

(Nov. 11, 1996)
Page 27—As discussed, the action of Santa indicating his crotch on the line "Right here, elfy" remains unacceptable.

(Nov. 15, 1996)
Page 33—Please substitute for George's line, "Holy crap!".

(Nov. 21, 1996)
Page 43—Lewis's reading of the 23rd Psalm as a source of humor will not be acceptable.

(Dec. 17, 1996)
Page 48—As discussed, please substitute "hooker" or
"prostitute" for "whore" in Beulah and Drew's dialogue.

(Jan. 9, 1997)
Page 6—Lewis's reference to "penis-enlarging" will not be
acceptable.

(Jan. 30, 1997)
Page 24—Stan's drug joke concerning "grass" is unacceptable.

(Feb. 13, 1997)
Page 41—"Piss" will not be acceptable for air.

From the "I can't believe these lines made it into the show"
file. A lot of the other lines in this chapter still made it into the
show, but these stand out in my mind.

(Apr. 6, 1995)
Mimi's line, "Can't you get laid here either?" will not be
acceptable.

(Aug. 24, 1995)
Page 27—Lewis's line, ". . . kiss . . . my ass" will not be
acceptable.

(Aug. 7, 1996)
Page 8—Mimi's line about 'f' and 'u' will not be acceptable.
(Mimi was starting to spell the word *fuck*.)

(Sept. 5, 1996. Our old high school principal discovers us
under the bleachers in the gym.)
Page 38—"Let's go, Dick Hertz" and "You too, Hunt, you

too, Lingus" will not be acceptable in the principal's dialogue.

Finally, we did a show toward the end of the '96–'97 season
that featured a character who was insane and wanted to kill me.
The character's name was Earl, and was played by David Cross
(from HBO's *Mr. Show*).

We received more angry letters complaining about this show
than just about any other show we've done. As I mentioned
before, most people were offended about the killer being crazy.
Here's Neil's attempt to save us, from a memo dated Jan. 31,
1997. Of course, he starts out with the usual:

> Please review the eleven uses of language found on pages
> 2, 9, 11, 15, 38, 40, 41, 42, 43, 48, and reduce to a maxi-
> mum of six noting only one use of "bastard" will be accept-
> able.

Then he goes on to the tricky stuff:

> Page 4—Here and again on pages 6 and 10, please substi-
> tute "stalk" or "haunt" for "kill" in Drew's lines.

> Page 5—Drew's reference to Earl having been "nuts" will
> not be acceptable. In addition, here and on page 9, please
> substitute "rehabilitation" for "therapy" in Earl's line to
> avoid linking his problem to mental illness.

> Page 7—Please substitute "inmate" for "patient" in Drew's
> line to avoid any inference to Earl having been in a mental
> institution. Earl should refer to himself as weird or strange
> rather than crazy.

> Page 9—Once again, Earl should mention "prison" instead
> of "therapy" as the source of his new anger technique.

Page 20—Please delete Earl's mention of "shock therapy."

Page 21—Drew's line, ". . . mood-altering drugs" will not be acceptable for broadcast. Lewis's use of "crazy" is unacceptable.

Page 52—Earl's use of a gun and the threat of death continues to be unacceptable. Use of the knife in a threatening manner would be an acceptable alternative to the gun.

And, like every memo from the Department of Broadcast Standards and Practices, it ends with the class-action-lawsuit-preventing statement:

We urge you to give attention to the inclusion of a realistic sampling of women, the disabled, ethnic minorities, and senior citizens in minor and nonspeaking roles in the script as well as in major roles.

Which just goes to show you that no matter how intrusive you think the Department of Broadcast Standards and Practices might be, the Legal Department is worse.

HARD

COPY

MADE

EZ

A Mountain Lion is on top of a hill fucking a Zebra. He's really going at it, when suddenly he sees Mrs. Mountain Lion on her way up the hill to catch him red-handed.

Thinking quickly, he grabs the Zebra by the shoulders and whispers in her ear, "Quick! Act like I'm killing you!"

When I first got my sitcom, I knew that because of my love of liquor and loose women, it would only be a matter of time before I ended up on a tabloid television show doing something stupid. And sure enough, I did.

It happened in New Orleans during Super Bowl weekend 1997. Even including the *Hard Copy* incident, it was one of the most fun weekends I've ever had in my life.

Technically, I was in New Orleans to do a stand-up concert the night before the game. In reality, it was a scam to come down to New Orleans and see the Super Bowl for free. The concert promoter paid for my plane ticket and hotel room, I talked ABC into giving me two seats on the fifty-yard line, and somehow I got invited to a special pregame party thrown by Coca-Cola, complete with passes to their private sky box to watch the game in case I didn't care for my fifty-yard line seats. Plus, I got paid a truckload of money for doing the concert. All for spending one hour on a stage telling the same jokes I always told before I got famous.

Do I know how to work the system, or what?

After my show was over, the promoter wanted to take me out to a bar. I don't always want to go straight to a bar after I do stand-up, but I do have that reputation and he was just trying to make me happy. It was also my first time in his hometown of New Orleans, so he wanted to show off the city's wild side. Not that he had to try very hard. New Orleans parties harder than any other city I've ever been in. How people keep a job in that town, I'll never know.

Now, besides being Super Bowl weekend, it was also the first weekend of Mardi Gras. The streets were packed with drunks like it was a Kennedy family reunion. Not just drunk, but falling-down sloppy drunk. Whooping, spinning, puking in the alley and going-back-for-more drunk. Everyone was acting like they were me when I was seventeen and using my fraternity brother's ID to buy 3.2 beer. It was insane.

The promoter took my manager and myself to a packed, seedy bar with a balcony that overlooked Bourbon Street. (Bourbon Street. Now there's a clue. The main party street is named after a gut-rotting liquor.) At least I thought the bar was seedy when I first got there. Having had a chance to visit most of the other shit holes on Bourbon Street that call themselves bars that weekend, I can say that comparatively, it was quite nice. Not that it matters. The main attraction of a bar on Bourbon Street during Mardi Gras isn't its decor. It's whether it has a balcony or not.

The balcony is where you stand with armfuls of cheap plastic beads that you can buy from the bar for about two dollars a bunch. (I'm only guessing at the price because the bar owner gave me my beads for free. Call me Mr. Scam.) The actual worth of the beads is about a nickel a strand, I figure. Anyway, you stand there with your nickel's worth of plastic beads, shake them at the thousand or so people standing in the street below you and yell as loudly as you can, "Show us your tits!!!" And women will willingly flash their bosoms at you, as long as you give them the beads.

Which comes down to: One flash of titty for a nickel.

I know this sounds unbelievable, but it's true. And, for the ladies, if you care to shake some beads and yell to a bunch of guys, "Show us your dicks!", they will. Everybody in New Orleans, it seems, is more than happy to display whatever sexual body part they've got, as long as they can get that nickel's worth of beads for their trouble.

So there's me, drunk off my ass, waving free beads around and yelling, "Show us your tits!" at the top of my lungs, whipping beads at strangers' heads and having the time of my life. If they would've blasted "Don't Stop Thinking About Tomorrow" by Fleetwood Mac over some loudspeakers, I would've been like Clinton at his first inauguration.

Now, down below in the drunken rabble, there's a bunch of people with beads, too. And they're yelling, "Show us your tits/dicks!" up at the people in the balconies. And the people in the balconies are more than happy to oblige. The invisible hand of free enterprise had turned the whole street into one big whip-it-out festival.

Beads were flying by my head at an alarming rate of speed, sometimes hitting me in the face and leaving welt marks that lasted until the next Monday. Of course, I wasn't whipping out my tits or anything else for them. They were being thrown for the very attractive young woman who was standing to my right, who was going above and beyond the call of duty as far as what you need to do to get a nickel's worth of beads in New Orleans.

Her blouse was up over her shoulders, her bra was off, her pants were down around her knees, and her panties were bunched around her thighs. Her boyfriend (?) stood behind her and cheered her on while he groped her. Guys sent her free drinks. Beads flew up from the streets and whapped her in the face. She couldn't get enough attention, or beads. Some sort of crazy bead addict, I guess.

The only time that the crowd tore their attention away from her (not counting the occasional tit-flasher in the street) was when the guy on the balcony across from us was getting a blow job.

That's right. I said a blow job. On a public balcony. With a thousand drunk people cheering him on. He was wearing a black tuxedo and had long brown hair. His girlfriend (?), a blonde with a great body and what turned out to be (after she sat up) a very pretty face, was in a tight-fitting black evening gown. If you're reading this buddy, congratulations.

Not only were the people in the street watching him and cheering him on, but so was everyone seated at the tables that surrounded his. Cheering, laughing, and throwing beads.

Then, the crowd began a chant, urging the gentlemen to return the favor. (The chant was deemed unprintable by the editors. Even for this book.) It wasn't one of the most suspenseful moments I've ever lived through, but certainly one of the most bizarre. He was on his knees in front of her faster than a sinner at a revival meeting. I still don't know how they did it. I mean, showing your body is one thing, but having sex in front of a crowd of strangers? I can't even use a public restroom if there's someone standing at the stall next to mine. The whole spectacle disturbed me enough to order two more beers and chug them.

Ten minutes later, I was thinking, "Maybe *I'm* the weird one. Maybe this is all normal behavior and I've just been living in a parallel universe. Am I ever going to find the cosmic wormhole that I fell into so I can get back home?," when a new group of women joined us on the balcony. Seeing new meat, the crowd began their shouts of, "Show us your tits! Show us your tits!"

The woman immediately to my left, whom I'll just call J. to protect her identity, kept shaking her head and mouthing the word *no*. "No?" I thought to myself. I didn't realize that such a word existed in New Orleans. This wasn't a city where people said "no." This was a city where people said "Sure! Why not?," and "You know what? I think I *will* have another!" But they never said "no," unless the question was, "Are you ready to stop partying and go home?"

"Why won't you show your tits?" I asked her.

"Are you kidding?" she exclaimed. "Oh, I could never! Someone will see me!"

I was astonished at her lack of logic. "No one's gonna see you," I slurred, waving a drunken arm at the bead-throwing mob below me.

"There's no way," she said.

"Show us your tits! Show us your tits!" screamed the multitude.

"Look," I reasoned with her. "No one knows you here. There's nothing but strangers down there, so if they do see you, so what? No one's gonna remember your tits out of all the tits that they've seen tonight. This is your one big chance to do something crazy and get away with it. No one's gonna know!" I was a drunken Johnnie Cochran, trying to convince a jury of one to vote her conscience. "If the weather permits, show your tits!"

"No," she said firmly.

Suddenly I realized. She must be from out of town. Of course. No woman in her right mind outside of New Orleans is going to flash her tits for just a nickel's worth of beads! If you don't believe me, try it where you live. Go to your local mall with an armful of plastic beads and ask women to show you their tits for them. Let me know what the food is like in jail.

No, this woman will only show her tits if she gets something of equal value in exchange. Adam Smith's invisible hand at work again, groping this woman's boobies.

"I'll give you a hundred bucks!" I announced loudly. This got her attention. I probably shouldn't have done it, but to tell the truth, I was tired of her acting like she was so above showing her tits when everyone else was.

"Really?" She was wary. I admit, I looked pretty drunk and disheveled by then and she probably didn't think I had a hundred on me.

"Swear to God. Show them your tits, I'll give you a hundred bucks." I took another swig of brain-cell-be-gone and tried to act calm.

"Show me the hundred first." I reached in my wallet and pulled out a hundred dollar bill.

"Oh my God. Really?" She and her friends were laughing and incredulous. She must have really needed the hundred. "You'll really give me that if I show my tits?"

"Show us your tits! Show us your tits!" The crowd was relentless.

"Yes," I assured her. "Sure as shit. Show your tits and it's yours."

"Give me the hundred first." I must've really looked out of it for this kind of distrustful treatment. First it's show me the hundred first, now it's give me the hundred first . . . I shoved the bill into her hand.

At first she looked at it as if she'd never seen a hundred dollar bill before. Then she and her girlfriends did a kind of giggly can-you-believe-it! dance while she looked at it some more. Then she shoved it into her pocket.

"Now c'mon," I reminded her. "I gave you the hundred, you have to show your tits." And she did.

She steeled herself, took a deep breath, and flashed the crowd to a rousing chorus of cheers, jiggling her tits for a full two seconds before stepping back from the balcony rail in a flush of excitement and nervous laughter. Beads flew. Drunks high-fived. Somewhere, an angel got its wings.

Two weeks later, it turns out someone had videotaped the whole thing, and we ended up on *Hard Copy*.

They showed me handing her the hundred (in slow motion, of course). Then they showed her flashing her tits while I stood next to her laughing and cheering. They called me "The Blue-Collar Tommy Lee," whatever that means. What does that make Tommy Lee? The Scourge of the Harvard Club?

I never saw it myself, but I heard about it from a friend of mine who saw it. And then, I heard about it from my publicist. Then from the crew on my show and everyone else I saw that week.

J. never saw it either, but heard about it from her father, who saw it and called her. Yikes. How do you talk your way out of that one?

I hope he's forgiven her for it. It's all my fault, after all. I'm the one who told her that no one would see her and that she could go ahead and do something wild and get away with it. I even gave her the hundred bucks.

I wonder if she and her father joke about it at family gatherings. "Remember when that Blue-Collar Tommy Lee boy got you to flash your titties to a crowd of strangers in New Orleans? Boy, was that funny! I just about fell off my chair."

I know that my friends and I laugh about it whenever it comes up. I've told this story to Jay Leno on *The Tonight Show*, I've told it in my stage act, and now it's a chapter in my book.

It turned out to be the best hundred dollars I ever spent.

TABLOIDS
MADE
EZ

 gorilla is walking through the jungle. He parts the bushes by the watering hole and sees a lion taking a drink of water with his butt sticking up in the air.

The gorilla thinks to himself that it would be really funny if he snuck up behind this "King of the Jungle" and slipped him the ol' Liberace. So the gorilla sneaks up on his tiptoes behind the lion, grabs him by the hips, and starts fucking him up his ass as hard as he can.

Then he pulls out and runs away, laughing his head off. He thinks it's the funniest thing he's ever done in his life, fucking the "King of the Jungle" up the ass.

The lion is pissed. "Rrrooooooaarrrrr!!!!" he says, and runs after the gorilla.

Now, the gorilla can't run very fast, and the lion keeps getting closer and closer, so the gorilla ducks into an empty safari camp, puts on a set of safari clothes with the pith helmet and everything, picks up a paper, sits down with the paper held up in front of his face, and makes like he's reading it.

Just then, the lion walks in. "Rrrrrooooooaarrrrr!!!!!!" he says. "Did you just see a big gorilla run through here?"

The gorilla starts shaking under the paper. "Uh, you mean the one that just f-fucked the lion up the ass?" he stutters.

The lion sits up with a start and says, "Jesus! It's in the paper already!?"

"DREW CAREY PEELS OFF 17 LBS. ON POTATO DIET."

That was the big scoop that the *Star* had on me in their February 18, 1997 issue. Ryan Stiles, who plays Lewis on *The Drew Carey Show,* was the first one to notice it. We were browsing through the tabloids at Los Angeles International Airport waiting for a flight to Cleveland to see the NBA All-Star game. I was sitting next to him eating a McDonald's sausage McMuffin with egg.

I have no idea why they published it, or where it came from, but there it was. There were also two photos of me claiming to show me before the weight loss and after. (The photos were taken from a couple of public functions that I had attended.) I weighed exactly the same in each photo, but the clothes were different, so I guess if you looked at them sideways you could maybe trick your eyes into thinking that I might have lost a pound or two. Except that I hadn't.

The article was typical of how the tabloids write about celebrities. Quotes from "a pal" and "a source." And then, to really make it sound legitimate, made-up quotes from the star himself, as told to the "pal."

> "It's a wacky diet, but it works for Drew," a source tells *Star*.
>
> "He's telling his costar Kathy Kinney that it could work for her. Drew is telling all his pudgy pals that it's the latest celebrity craze."

Never happened. Never said it. Never would say it. "Hey pudgy pal, this potato diet is the latest celebrity craze!"

> Drew is so thrilled with the eating plan he's designed . . . that he's telling pals he'll soon be Hollywood's hottest new hunk.
>
> "In a few weeks I'll be looking so good you'll all be calling me the 'Spud Stud,' " he boasts.

No, I don't. I was never even on this stupid diet. I haven't lost any weight at all this past year.

It goes on to give *Star* readers an "exclusive" one-day sample of recipes from "Drew's potato diet," along with advice like ". . . Drew prefers a low-fat vegetable spray," and "Drew also recommends lots of water—he downs eight glasses a day . . . ," and "He also warns against eating anything within four hours of bedtime."

I think that the genesis for the story came while I was actually trying to lose weight during last season, and mentioned, in passing, when a group of people were standing around the food table that we have on the stage, that I thought that potatoes were a great food to eat if you were trying to lose weight.

Next thing you know, someone is calling the *Star* and selling them a story about how I've lost seventeen pounds eating nothing but potatoes all day long. And, because the tabloids are so picky about their editorial content, they printed it. Along with made-up quotes and recipes.

Now, don't get me wrong. All my friends and I got a lot of laughs out of the story, and it didn't hurt me personally or professionally. I'm just telling you about it so you can have an example of how the tabloids operate.

They lie.

And if they don't make up a lie themselves, they'll print whatever lies someone else has told them.

You know what it's like being in the tabloids? It's like being gossiped about in junior high. If you've ever had a rumor about you floating around when you were in school, you know exactly how it feels. For instance, some guy says he slept with you when he didn't, so now you're the school slut. How are you going to prove that you're not? You can't. That's how it is being in the *National Enquirer, Star*, or *The Globe*. Only it's worse, because of the lengths that they'll go to to find something bad to say about somebody.

And this is coming from someone who the tabloids have been nice to. There's only one story that I wish they hadn't printed, but oh well. That's life when you're on TV.

What happened was that one of the tabloids put out the word that I had gotten "secretly engaged" to a girl I had dated, who meant a lot to me, and that I was very close to, but was in the middle of breaking up with; so their timing couldn't have been worse. Legitimate magazines and newspapers that picked it up kept calling my publicist for confirmation of the story. My mom called me and wondered why I left her out of the loop. It made it harder for me to get a date.

But even in the stories that have been "celebrity friendly," they misquote people, or make up feelings that they imagine you might have had about an event in your life, or they get dates or names wrong. It's just amazing to me all the mistakes they make. Then, when they do get an important celebrity story (the *Enquirer*, for example, had some great scoops during the O. J. Simpson trial), they wonder why people question their credibility.

Now, they don't always make stuff up to hurt you. Like I said, they've written mostly very flattering things about me, but a lot of them have been lies. Flattering lies, but lies nonetheless. They said I gave a heckler at the Improv a ride home. Nice if I did, but I didn't. They said I gave $5,000 to a guy I did a charity event for. Again, it makes me sound swell, but I didn't do it. See? Even in articles where they want to make you sound like a great guy they make stuff up. Maybe they don't know that journalism isn't supposed to be such a creative field of work.

For example, *The Globe* ran a story about me in their February 25, 1997 issue entitled "Drew Carey's Secret World." It was full of childhood photos of me that a freelance photographer from Detroit talked my mother into giving him.

Even though it clearly wasn't a story where they were out to get me (they were actually quite complimentary in the article, and I thank them for it), they guessed about my weight (250 pounds—I've never been close to being that heavy), quoted me as saying that losing my father was ". . . the most devastating, frightening thing ever to happen to me," and threw in a couple of other things that I never said. (Don't get me wrong, losing my father was bad, but it certainly wasn't the most devastating and frightening thing that ever happened to me.)

Now, this was an article whose intent was to make me sound endearing, and I actually liked it. But they still made stuff up. Imagine if a tabloid hated me.

I feel fortunate that the tabloids have treated me pretty decently in my short career. But the fact that it does happen is enough to worry me. Is the cute blonde that says she wants to have sex with me being paid $75,000 by *The Globe* to tape-record the encounter? Can I throw my mail in the trash like a normal person or do I have to buy a shredder so that someone from a tabloid doesn't grab it from my garbage can? (They already know where I live, even though my house isn't even listed under my name.) Can I go to a strip club with my friends and have a good time like I'm used to? Or is a tabloid reporter going to show up and make me out to be some kind of sex maniac for doing what a million other guys do every day without anyone blinking an eye?

Even my dates aren't immune. The girl that they thought I was engaged to was constantly harassed by tabloid reporters. Not to get information about me, but about her.

They called her and said they were from AT&T. ("We'd like to confirm a call you made. Can you spell your last name please?") They called her and said that they were from a production company and wanted to hire her but they needed some information first. They found out her mother's name and called her mother. They called her grandmother. They called her estranged father. They called her mother's neighbors and people that she went to school with. They called her and said that they were from ABC to try and get information from her. They followed her to school in a van with no license plates, and questioned people there. They rang her doorbell and waited outside her apartment for her, trying to get her to talk to them. All because of a false story that we were engaged.

Then, after all that, one of them (*The Globe*) printed a picture of us together and got her name wrong! Her name is Elena (pronounced e-LAY-na), and they called her "Ellen." See what I mean? They're sneaky and sloppy all at the same time.

That's not to say that they're not entertaining. They are. I read them all the time. But I know that they're mostly lies and half-truths, and you should know that, too.

Am I worried about them taking some kind of revenge against me for writing this chapter? For even voicing the smallest complaint against their journalistic credibility after they've been so nice to me? No. Once everyone else I've insulted in this book gets through with me, there won't be anything left. They won't even find the body.

FAQ.COM

man walks by a cafe that has a sign in its window: *PIANO PLAYER WANTED*. He grabs the sign, walks in the cafe and says to the manager, "I play the piano. I'd like to have the piano player's job."

The manager says, "Well, let's hear you play first."

The man sits down and plays the most beautiful song the manager has ever heard. The manager is crying for joy at the beauty of the song.

"That song is so wonderful!" he exclaims. "But I've never heard it before. I must know what it's called!"

"Well," the man says, "it's an original tune. I wrote it myself. It's called 'The I've Got Dog Shit on My Pecker and Rover's Done Run Off Blues.'"

"Oh," says the manager, taken somewhat aback. "Well, do you know any other songs?"

"Sure!" says the man, and begins to play a song even more beautiful than the first one.

The manager is once again beside himself with emotion, swept away even more than he was by the first song.

"Oh my God!" he shouts. "Never have I seen such artistry! And again, a song I've never heard! I must know the name of this beautiful song!"

The man says, "Thank you. It's another original tune that I wrote myself. It's called 'The Blow Your Brother, Fuck a Goat, and Tell Me That You Love Me Waltz, in D Minor.'"

The manager thinks for a moment and says, "Look, I like the way you play piano, and I'm going to hire you. But only on one condition: Don't ever tell my customers the names of the songs that you're playing."

The man agrees and comes in to play that very night. The crowd is stunned by his mastery of the piano and the beauty of his compositions. He gets a standing ovation at the end of each one of his songs.

At the end of an hour and a half, the man has to go to the bathroom, so he stops playing and announces to the audience, "Ladies and Gentlemen, I'm going to take a short break now. Please stay and enjoy a drink, and I'll be back to play again for you in fifteen minutes."

After he pees, he forgets to zip up his zipper. On his way out of the bathroom another man stops him and says "Hey, do you know your zipper's undone and your cock's hanging out?"

The man says, "Know it? I wrote it!"

Ever since I was a kid, I've had a lot of questions about certain things concerning show business. Not important things, just things. And, now that I have the answers to these nagging questions, I thought I'd pass them on to you.

I've also included answers to questions that I always get asked by fans and friends. And, you're my friend . . . aren't you?

WHAT'S IT LIKE BEING ON TV?

Some genius once said that show business is like high school with money, and that's exactly what it's like. And, since we've all been to high school, everything that I've experienced being a TV star, most of you have experienced yourself.

Ever been gossiped about at school (or at work)? You know what it's like to be in the tabloids.

Ever been in a popular clique? An unpopular one? You know what it's like to work on a hit show, or one that's failing.

Ever resented the cheerleaders for no other reason than that they're popular? Welcome to Warner Brothers! Home of *ER, Friends,* and every other show that's more popular and profitable than yours is.

Ever hung out with the cheerleaders and gotten a big kick out of it, because they're so good-looking and cool? Welcome to a corporate party at Warner Brothers! Home of *ER* and *Friends* and all those other great shows. Warner Brothers kicks ass, man.

Ever been beaten up after school? Hey, you're "Frasier," flipping over his sports car and going into rehab!

Bad report card? Welcome to bad ratings.

Bad report card and your parents don't care? Welcome to bad ratings on The WB.

Ever gotten married? Was it a big wedding? Hey, welcome to being a celebrity! You know what it's like to have people you don't even know look at you funny all day long. Every eye on you, trying not to stare. People talking about your chances behind your back: "How long do you think it'll last? Gee, her hair looks stupid. Wasn't he married before?" Every day is like that. I can't take off the stupid wedding dress.

Of course, after time you do get used to the clothes and start to not notice them much anymore. Except once in a while, you'll go somewhere you shouldn't go or do something you really shouldn't do, and realize too late, "Shit. I'm still in my wedding dress!"

However, there are some things about being on TV that I don't think the average person can relate to. Like the money. The money is ridiculous, and you'll never hear me complaining about an overpaid sports star again. My manager calls it "Stupid Money." It's the kind of money that Jerry Seinfeld and Tim Allen make. It's the kind of money that I *want* to make. After that, I want to take off the wedding clothes (if I can), and disappear.

Then, when you get the money, everyone wants to buy you stuff. Take Nike, for example. On the very day that my new show was announced as being picked up by ABC for the fall schedule, a woman from Nike put her card in my hand, and I haven't paid for sneakers since. I have Nike shoes, shorts, T-shirts, running gear, hiking boots, everything. They just send it to me. I don't even have to ask. As long as I wear it, and I wear it all the time, it keeps on coming.

Nike, Nike, Nike.

There. I should be getting more new shoes any day now.

(I also love Budweiser, Pepsi, and The Gap, if anyone cares. Oh, and one of those cool new BMW Z3s.)

I also get invited to movie premiers all the time, which is really cool except when the movie sucks. Because after the movie is over, people from *Entertainment Tonight* and *Showbiz Today* want to interview you and ask you what you thought of it. Sometimes, I'd like to tell the truth and say, "Yo, bro', this movie sucks, ya know what I'm sayin'? Yo'," but I can't because I'm drinking their beer. So I lie. Everybody lies at those things. Even after people saw *Speed 2*, they said, "Oh, it was great!" Never believe a review from a celebrity coming out of a movie premier.

One time I didn't have to lie was when I got to see the premier of *Independence Day*. I loved it, and own a copy of it on laser disc. The only bad part was, I got stuck doing interviews outside the theater for so long that by the time I got inside, the only decent seats left were in the center of the very front row. I had to watch the whole movie looking straight up. The good news was that, technically, I was the first one to see the movie.

WHAT DOES THE "GRIP" DO?

Well, on my show, he plays chess with the star. On other shows, and in movies, he's kind of the all-around handyman. The Grips do a lot of little stuff like moving big set pieces in between scenes, propping up the phony set walls and stuff, and holding the ladder for the lighting guys. A little of this, a little of that. They all keep a Union Rule Book in their back pockets. The "Key Grip" is the main Grip guy.

The Grips, the Electricians and Lighting Guys, the Camera Operators, the Sound Crews, the Prop People and Set Dressers, the Builders, the Painters; they're the only ones that do what could be called honest work on the stage, and they're also the hardest people to impress. None of them could give a real rat's ass if you're a TV star or not, as long as they're getting a paycheck, and if you try pulling a star trip on them, be prepared for a lot of rolling eyes and death threats.

WHAT IS A "TRANSPORTATION CAPTAIN"?

He's the guy in charge of the guys that transport all of the film and equipment to and from the stage. In any other job, they're truck drivers. In show-biz, they're "Transportation Captains." All the transportation guys are great at slinging bullshit and knowing if the coffee is fresh. They always know ahead of everyone else on the lot whether or not a show is picked up or canceled, and 99 percent of the time, they're right.

WHAT IS "ADR"?

I forget what it stands for (Automated Digital Recording? Automatic Dialogue Replacement? All Day Re-recording shit? Arrgggh, Dammit! Rrrrr?), but it's a huge pain in the ass. It used to be called "looping."

You have to stand in a big room with a movie screen and a microphone. Then, you have to dub your own voice over sound flubs from the taping while you watch yourself on the screen. It has to exactly match the way your mouth was moving, and it's a royal pain. Everyone on my show knows how much I hate it, and they try to avoid making me do it as much as they can.

If you want to know what ADR is like, have a friend look at you and read something from the paper, but just moving his or her lips, not making any sound. Read the same thing your friend is reading out loud, trying to match their lip movements exactly. It has to be exact, or you have to do it over and over until you want to punch the producer that called you in there.

WHAT IS A "FOLEY ARTIST"?

They're not really used much in sitcoms, but I've always wondered, and I'll bet you do, too. Every time I used to see "Foley

Artist" in the credits of a movie I'd wonder, "What the hell does that guy do?" A Foley Artist is a man or woman that makes sound effects. Punching sounds, walking sounds, falling-down sounds, galloping horses, that kind of stuff. Like they used to do on radio. I heard that they're named after a guy named "Foley" who was the first really good Foley Artist.

WHY ARE THERE SO MANY PRODUCERS LISTED IN THE CREDITS OF A SITCOM?

Good question. Who the hell knows, really? I think that it's because "Hey baby, I'm a producer" gets you laid more than "Hey baby, I'm a writer."

Many of the producer titles (Associate Producer, Producer, Supervising Producer) are nothing more than writing titles that are given out to writers like the army gives out ranks. It's a way of telling people your spot in the writing pecking order and how much you get paid.

There's a lot of confusing titles for writers. Take "Story Editor" for example. It's just a salary bump up from the beginning position of "Staff Writer." A Story Editor doesn't edit any stories at all. All it means is that the Executive Producer felt sorry for a staff writer and wanted to give them a raise without spending too much money on it. (The next step up is "Executive Story Editor." It might as well be called "King of the Story Editors" for all it matters.)

After that, it's all "something-Producer," all the way up to "Executive Producer." Except that they're all really only writers. Got it?

Other production titles have to do with hiring camera and sound crews, budgeting the money, and things like that. Boring, un-creative, technical stuff. Before you sleep with a producer, find out what kind they are, because some producers have no power at all. You could be going to bed with someone who is nothing more than a bean counter and couldn't get you a part on the show if he or she wanted to.

Now, in the sitcom world, the Executive Producer is the man or woman in charge of running the show. In fact, since so many stars (like me eventually) demand Executive Producer titles to boost their egos and salary, the real Exec Producer is usually referred to by the nickname "Show Runner." E.g., "Who's the Show Runner over at *Roseanne* this year?"

He or she is like the CEO of a company. They are in charge of the writer's room, mostly, but are consulted on everything else about the show, no matter how minor. Bruce Helford is the Executive Producer of my show. (If he's like the CEO, then I'm like the Board of Directors.) We created the show together and have a great relationship. He is as much my friend as he is my partner.

On some sitcoms, you'll see that the star is the Executive Producer. Now, how can that be, you might wonder? How can the star of the show be in the writer's room, over in editing, sitting in on casting decisions, and rehearsing all day, all at the same time? The answer is, they can't. It's just another title that they demand from the studio so the public will think that they're really powerful and smart. Then they'll do an interview about how bad their writers are (if they even know their writers' names) and how they came up with every good idea on their own. Well, let me tell you something: Anyone who thinks that Roseanne writes her own scripts probably thinks that Bill Gates writes all the programs for Microsoft. That is, if they know who Bill Gates is.

Right now, I get two paychecks from Warner Brothers. One for being the star, and one for being the Supervising Producer (a writing credit, because I'm in the writer's room part-time.) I might ask for an Executive Producer credit on my show soon, just because I can.

HEY! ISN'T IT YOUR SHOW? DOESN'T WHAT YOU SAY GO ALL THE TIME?

Well, yes and no. It could, but then I'd get stuck dealing with a lot of detail stuff that would take away from rehearsal, and I need all the rehearsal time I can get. When you have people as competent and good as the people I have working on a show, why try and do their jobs? Sometimes they're wrong, and sometimes I'm wrong, but nobody tries to pull a power trip about it. It's more of a collegial work environment than a Mad Queen ruling by fear.

I really like it that way; letting everyone do the best job that they can without me getting in the way. I know that if I wanted to, I could fire everybody and take credit for all of their ideas, and put my name on any script I wanted for a writing credit I didn't deserve. I mean, I'm the star. But what would be the point? I'm trying to put on the best television show I can, not win first prize in an asshole contest.

WHEN PRODUCERS HAVE MEETINGS, WHAT HAPPENS?

Well, I don't know what Steven Spielberg, or Joel Schumacher, or any of those other so-called "Producers" do at their meetings, but in sitcom television, a "production meeting" goes something like this: We get together on Wednesday mornings, the start of our work week. Most of the country starts work at eight or nine—we start at eleven. We also have coffee and donuts.

Now, stars of sitcoms never go to these, and I don't feel guilty if I miss them, but I go most all of the time. I feel like I have to, to help earn the Supervising Producer paycheck that I get.

What the production meeting is, is all of the Prop guys and Set Decorators and Wardrobe ladies deciding what they're going to need for that week's script. Bruce Helford, Deborah Oppenhiemer (our main budget and hiring Producer lady), and I go because we have to.

The meetings are scintillating, and are chock full of witty repartee like this:

"Page seven, Drew grabs an umbrella."

"What kind of umbrella?"

"Dunno, doesn't say."

"Maybe one of those collapsible ones?"

"No, Drew would probably have the long kind."

"What color?"

"I don't know. Drew, do you have a favorite color?"

Then it's my turn to earn my Supervising Producer money. "Blue, I guess. I dunno. But you better make it black. Black is more businesslike. Right, Bruce?"

"Um, yeah sure. Black. Black is fine," says Bruce, wiping the sleep from his eyes.

"Uh, Bru-u-u-ce . . . ," Deborah will coo, "we had a request from an umbrella company in Cleveland to have us use one of their umbrellas on the show. Maybe we can use one of theirs, if it's okay with Drew. It's got the Cleveland Indians' logo on it."

"Well, we'd have to clear that with Major League Baseball," someone else adds. "Can we get someone to call the baseball people about that?"

"All right," says the assistant director, who chairs the meeting. "We'll call Major League Baseball about the umbrella issue, and if not we'll get a black one as a back up."

"You know, we have some blue ones just laying around in the back."

"Hmm. Blue wouldn't be so bad. That was your first choice, wasn't it Drew?"

"Um, well either way, really. Blue or black."

"We can get blue. It wouldn't be a problem."

It's like that for an hour. Everybody hates these meetings. If we had a choice, we'd all rather drive across the country with a broken radio.

WHAT'S YOUR WORK SCHEDULE LIKE?

We start rehearsals on Wednesdays, and tape on Tuesdays.

Three weeks on, one week off. Twenty-four shows a year. Although, during the hiatus week (and a couple of nights a week otherwise), I do hang around in the writer's room and put in my two cents. (Gotta earn that Supervising Producer money.)

I figure I work about fifty-five or sixty hours a week, not counting interviews and promotional work. But I never complain because I know that however many hours I work, the writers work more. And they don't get all the free Nike stuff that I do.

ARE YOU REALLY ON AOL?

Yes, but I hardly ever sign on anymore, so don't expect an answer if you write me. When the show first started, I took the screen name "DrewCShow" to answer questions and criticisms in our *Drew Carey Show* folder in the ABC section of AOL. People also wrote me e-mail, and I answered as many as I could. Then, when the show got more popular, it just got to be too much to handle so I stopped signing on with that name. When I started spending three hours a day just answering e-mail, I decided to stop before I went crazy. I haven't looked at any of my e-mail on that account for months, even though I still keep it.

ARE THOSE YOUR REAL GLASSES?

Yes. The original frames from my first days of stand-up were from the Marine Corps Reserves. I wore them all the time, never knowing how dorky I really looked in them. Then, I broke those and bought frames similar to those at an antique clothing store in Cleveland. Then, those broke (hit in the face with a football, slept on them, you name it), and the prop guys at my show had to send them to England to have an exact duplicate of the frames made for me.

I always wear them when I perform, but not always in real life. I have a pair of wire rims that I wear mostly during the day when I don't feel like being stopped by anybody. I still get stopped, but at least with the wire rims, people have to look twice to make sure it's me, and by that time, I'm gone. I also wear contact lenses sometimes for the same reason.

ARE YOU AS GOOD IN BED AS WOMEN SAY YOU ARE?

Better. Spread the word.

DOESN'T YOUR MOTHER GET UPSET AT ALL OF THE BAD LANGUAGE THAT YOU USE?

I don't care. I've got bills to pay.

YOUR SHOW SUCKS. HOW DO YOU SLEEP AT NIGHT?

On a bed full of money.

MY NIPPLE'S GOT A HOLE IN IT AND I MIGHT DROWN

Two flies are sitting on a piece of shit. One fly cuts a fart. The other fly looks at him and says, "Hey! I'm eatin' here!"

I have a pierced nipple. The right one. I used to have both nipples pierced, but the left one was put in too close to the skin and it hurt all the time, so I took it out.

I know it sounds painful, and it is when you first get it done. But other than that, it's great. Especially when you're having sex. (Okay, only when you're having sex.) In fact, the left one will probably be re-pierced by the time this book hits the stores. It's always better if you have two.

I got the original piercing done in Florida after I had filmed the pilot for *The Drew Carey Show*. I wasn't sure of anything right then, except that if the pilot didn't sell, I wasn't going to do any more sitcom work. I really felt that if the show didn't sell, I would just concentrate on doing stand-up and that's all. Or maybe get a job. Or maybe . . . who knows?

It's a weird feeling, doing a television pilot. Especially if you're the star and co-creator like I was. It's like it's all on your head if it fails. I felt like if it failed, Bruce Helford (who I wrote it with) would get another writing job with no problem, but what would happen to me?

I could just see me being introduced at a comedy club: "Ladies and Gentlemen, please welcome the failure who couldn't even write a funny sitcom, something he used to think a monkey could do."

That is, if I decided to still do stand-up comedy. I could write . . . I could take more acting lessons and try to get character roles in the movies . . . maybe the show will get picked up for the season, maybe it won't. . . . My mind was a mess back then as I drove across the country. I was driving to clear my head, and all I could do was obsess on my uncertain future.

It's like you're at a crap game, and on your biggest roll, the dice go in slow motion. For months, you watch them spin and roll and bounce around, waiting for them to land so you know if you're a winner or a loser. Total limbo.

So I let a stripper talk me into getting my nipples pierced. It didn't take her much to convince me. It doesn't take women much to talk me into doing anything, really. She was beautiful, I'd seen her naked . . . that's all it usually takes.

I don't think that the executives at Warner Brothers and ABC were too happy about it at first, even though they never said so. But, now that they've gotten to know me and I've become friends with most of them, I think they're just relieved I didn't pierce my face.

I almost said "shaved my head and pierced my face," but then I remembered, I did shave my head later on that summer. Just out of boredom. A shaved head and pierced nipples. I looked . . . incredibly gay. All I needed was a leather vest and a pair of work boots, and I could've been somebody's Daddy Bear. But you can't always judge people on their looks. Just because a guy has a shaved head, pierced nipples, and doesn't have sex with women doesn't make him gay. It just makes him down on his luck.

When I shaved it, I already knew that the show had been picked up for the Fall season and I thought, "Oh, no problem. It'll grow back by the time we start filming in August."

What I forgot was that we had to film promo spots for the show in July.

I ended up having to pay $1,200 out of my own pocket for a toupee so I could film those stupid promos. Twelve hundred fucking dollars.

And I only got to wear it the one day.

MY SHORT, HAPPY LIFE

**A** man is sitting at home when he hears a knock on the door. He opens the door and sees a snail sitting there on the porch. He picks up the snail, and throws it as far as he can.

Three years later, there's a knock on the door. The man opens the door. There sits the same snail.

The snail says, "What the hell was that all about?"

★   ★   ★

This is the part I've been dreading.

Don't worry, it'll be quick. It'll be quick because I can't stand writing about my life history like this and want to get it over with.

For one thing, I don't think that I'm old enough or accomplished enough to do any kind of lengthy autobiographical writing. I mean, I'm only a comedian in a sitcom for crying out loud. And my show's not even at the top of the ratings. It's only in the top twenty. I haven't done anything important or life changing, and if my show had never made it on the air, no one would've missed it; the world would've still kept on turning.

Plus, I personally can't stand celebrity autobiographies that go on and on, page after page, about their troubled childhoods and substance abuses. Talking about them is one thing, but sheesh, spare us the whole book, will ya?

However, I know a lot of people love reading about the lives of their favorite stars, and are even inspired by the way that those same stars overcame their troubles. So this chapter is for you people. You'll get to know more about one of your favorite TV celebrities, and I'll get your cash.

Sounds like a good deal to me.

And, as a bonus (and to make up for the lack of information in this chapter), I've included some photos of myself in my younger years and a stunning revelation. No extra charge.

I'm starting this section on May 22, 1997. One day before my thirty-ninth birthday (I was born in 1958 in Cleveland, Ohio, the youngest of three sons).

I don't know what it is about my birthday. I always try to just ignore it, never throwing a party for myself or doing anything special. But I still end up thinking about how my life would've been different if I would've done one thing, or never had done another.

It used to depress me, because I would think everything I did up until then in my life was a mistake. But, since I've been on TV and gotten a small amount of fame and money, the memories of the times in my life where I had my biggest screwups are now somehow comforting.

There's a few things that I could make a lot of sad noises about, but I won't. Maybe another book, another time. I'll mention them (very quickly), because they did have a great effect on what kind of man I am today, and then I'll move along, so as to spare you some sap.

The first thing was that my father died when I was eight years old. It wasn't sudden. He'd been in and out of Deaconess Hospital (the same hospital I was born in) ever since I could remember, and I still have very few memories of him when he wasn't sick.

He had blood clots in his legs, a couple of strokes, a heart attack or two . . . then a brain tumor finally got to him. When I was seven, he had an eye removed in an effort to get at the tumor. I thought it was cool because he wore a patch. He even let me look into the socket once, and showed me how he could breath through the hole where his eye used to be.

Those are the kinds of memories I have of my old man. I remember ambulances taking him away from the house. I remember seeing him in the hospital and smelling that awful old blood smell on him. I remember him coming home from the hospital. I remember the funeral.

What I don't remember is him taking me to the ball game or playing catch, or any of the other things he would've liked to have done with me had he been healthy. For all I know, he did do those things with me, I just don't remember them.

He was only forty-five when he died.

A year after he passed on, when I was nine, I was sexually

molested. Hey, that ought to sell some books, huh? Not even my family knows that.

I didn't tell anyone that it happened. I was raised in a time where everyone thought that sex was dirty, and nobody talked about it, ever. Not to a nine-year-old anyway.

And, because it was sexual, I was embarrassed by it. Just like everyone else in America seems to be taught to be embarrassed by sex. Sexually oriented magazines and movies are regularly denounced by politicians and other meddlesome types from each end of the political spectrum even to this day. Why? Because they're about sex, that's why. And to those people, sex is bad. Just about the only thing that you can get radical feminists and conservative Christians to agree on is that decent beat-off material should be harder to find than ice cubes in a desert. The drumbeat was, and still is, if it has to do with sex, hide it, deny it, and don't talk about it. So I didn't.

Never told a therapist, or a teacher, or a minister, or a family member. All my life I lived with it buried inside me, like *Playboys* hidden under a mattress. Every once in a while it would come up in my mind, but I would quickly force it back down, because somehow I knew it would make me take an honest look at how badly certain things in my life had been fucked up because of it.

It was only a few years ago that I even figured out for myself how much being molested affected me. Jesus, have I had some fucked-up times because of that one summer when I was a boy. You wouldn't think that something that happened so few times could leave such a big ripple in your psychic pond, but it does. It's just amazing.

I've read quite a bit about the sexual abuse of boys in the past five years, trying to figure out how to get rid of all the negative feelings about myself that came with it. Every book has these gruesome case histories about someone's loving grandfather taking them out behind the garage and making them blow him, or someone else's trusted neighbor anally raping them on a camping trip. What happened to me wasn't quite up to that level, and, thank God, didn't involve a relative. It was still bad, though.

I know this doesn't give you a lot of details of what happened to me exactly, and I don't want it to. In fact, after this book is done, I don't want to talk about it in public ever again. I don't want to make a living off it. I've dealt with it and don't want to bring up this ultimate bummer to the front of my psyche every time I do an interview.

How I dealt with it could take up an entire book of its own, so forgive me for not going into details. But, if something like this has happened to you, please get some help. A therapist, a book, anything to start a healing process so that you can enjoy your life more. There's a lot of guilt and self-hate that results from being sexually abused or molested. You don't need to live with it for the rest of your life.

I needed to mention it because I believe it had a great deal to do with why I had such a severe case of depression over the years. It's not directly responsible for my depression, but it was another big ripple in the pond.

It's been widely reported already, but I tried to commit suicide two different times in my life. Once, when I was eighteen and just finishing up my freshman year in college, and again a few years later when I was living in Las Vegas. Both times I took sleeping pills.

Let me tell you something about my attempted suicides that I don't think I ever mentioned to any reporter. The bright side of attempted suicide.

The best thing to come out of me taking those pills and feeling so bad about myself was that now, I'm not afraid of what anyone thinks of me. A lot of people (especially celebrities) stop themselves from doing all kinds of things that they would like to do because they're afraid of what people will think of them. Not me.

I let myself do whatever I want, with whomever I want, whenever I want, and don't care if anybody likes it or not. I'm not talking about being rude. I try not to do that, even though my neighbor who's complained about my stereo more than a few times might disagree. I'm talking about living a life without caring if people like the way you have your fun.

I got my nipples pierced, just for the hell of it. I date strippers, because I finally can. I let myself drink and gamble without feeling guilty about it. I take more chances. I don't have to try to hide what the press calls "my wild side" because I don't care who knows. I should be dead by now. But because I'm not, and because God gave me a second and third chance to accept being alive and imperfect, that's what I'm going to be: Alive— taking chances, making mistakes, and enjoying every minute of it.

So there. Now you have it. I had a childhood with no father, I was sexually molested when I was a boy, and I tried to kill myself twice.

Boy, is the money gonna roll in.

Don't get the idea that I had an unhappy childhood, though. I thought it was great. There were a lot of positive influences in my life, and I'm grateful for all of them.

Music was one of the main ones. Looking back, I count all of those hours I was forced to practice by my mother as some of my happiest memories.

When I was in first grade, a man came to our house from the

local music store to sell us lessons. Naturally, because I was only five, no one told me he was coming, so I had to make up my mind on the spot about what instrument I wanted to take up. I chose the accordion.

My oldest brother Neal wanted to learn guitar, because all the R&B artists that he loved played the guitar. My second-oldest brother Roger chose drums because all the rock bands that he liked had a cool drummer. I was the last one to pick, being the youngest of the three children, and I chose the accordion because I'd just seen some nerd playing one on *The Gene Carroll Show,* a locally televised talent search that the family watched after church on Sundays. I didn't know any better.

In fourth grade, I quit the accordion and took up trumpet so I could be in the band. Even then, accordion players had to scratch for gigs.

I played seriously through my years at Rhodes High School, but then stopped taking lessons after my mom pressured me into quitting a polka band I had gotten into. I was only sixteen years old at the time, and she didn't want me playing in bars every weekend, which is what would've happened. I didn't see myself studying trumpet in college, and wasn't good enough anyway, so I quit taking lessons. I reasoned that if I couldn't play for money in a band, why bother?

However, I did continue to play in college a little bit. I joined the marching band at Kent State University for one year because a friend of mine was in it and told me that the parties were really great. I also got into the Kent State pep band that performed at the basketball games because we got to sit behind the cheerleaders. Everyone else in the pep band was a music major. Music this, jazz that, minor seventh chords, blah blah blah. I was only there to catch a flash of cheerleader panty while they jumped up and down ten feet in front of us.

Last year, on a lark, I bought a brand-new Bach Stradivarius trumpet. I also bought an extremely expensive accordion that I can hook up to a MIDI board to make it sound like an orchestra if I want it to. I'm not near as good (on the trumpet, especially) as I used to be. In fact, I suck, but I don't care. I play strictly for my own enjoyment and no one else's, and look forward to playing music more now than at any other time in my life.

I also sang in the choir until I got to high school. The year before, when I was in ninth grade at Mooney Junior High, I starred as Frederick, the pirate apprentice in Gilbert and Sullivan's *The Pirates of Penzance.*

The experience was not unlike what I've been going through being the star of my own TV show. Kids I didn't know all that well started saying hello to me in the hall, cute girls I never talked to before were passing me love notes, and no matter where I went, I always felt like people were staring at me.

After that, I never took choir again. I have a lousy singing voice anyway.

To get out of high school early, I only needed to take senior English so I took it in the summer after eleventh grade and graduated early. You can see the picture of me holding my diploma in the front yard of my house. I weighed 123 pounds.

Two months later I was at Kent State. No reason. I just figured I should go to college, so I went. It's amazing all the decisions in my life that were made like that, never thinking about why or if I really wanted it. I just did stuff because it was the thing to do.

"Hey, you just got out of high school, you should go to college," I reasoned. I didn't know what I wanted to be, what to major in, or what business I had being in college in the first place; I just knew that after high school, that's where people usually went. Same thing with parts of my stand-up career.

"Hey, you should be on a sitcom." Why? Because stand-up comics are on sitcoms, that's why. "Hey, you're a comic, you want do *The Tonight Show*? Hey, nice *Tonight Show* spot, you want your own cable special? Hey, you had a cable special, you want to be on a sitcom? Hey, you're on a sitcom, you want to write a book?" Sure, why not? That's why I joined a fraternity. "Hey, you're in college, you should be in a fraternity."

I will say, though, that making important life decisions like that has mostly backfired on me. ("Hey, you finally found a girl to have sex with. You want her to be your girlfriend?") The only things I really did well at were things that I decided I needed and wanted, and then planned out. My first *Tonight Show* appearance was one of those things. As was *The Drew Carey Show*. The first sitcom project I was involved in was a "Hey, you want to star in a sitcom?" type thing, and was a total disaster. The script was terrible, I thought the executive producer was a total dick, and I got fired from it in the middle of the LA riots. It never saw the light of day. I did it for the same reason I did almost every other thing in my life. Because it was there.

Luckily, when it came to joining a fraternity, I rolled a seven. The friends that I made back then have been lifelong, and the lessons I learned were invaluable. I'll admit that I haven't had a chance to use what I learned at our chapter meetings about parliamentary procedure, and I've never again had to make a bong out of a toilet paper roll, but who knows? Someday I might.

To give you an idea of what a dork I was back then, I'll tell you this quick story:

At my first fraternity rush party (for Delta Tau Delta, which I later joined), I was asked what my hobbies were. In high school I was really into these complicated war games from companies like Avalon Hill that sometimes took months to play out. Real high-end nerd stuff. (There were no personal computers back then.)

I also mentioned that I liked playing Monopoly and Risk.

So, just to be polite, and so he could change the subject to chicks or sports or something normal, the fraternity guy says, "Well, that sounds great. I'd really like to see those sometime."

I was so clueless, that at the next beer-keg blow-out rush party for Delta Tau Delta, I showed up at the door with about five of these war games under my arm, plus Monopoly and Risk, thinking that these guys were going to sit around with me eating pizza and conquering the world instead of getting drunk and trying to pick up girls.

I don't know how I even was asked to join Delta Tau Delta. I didn't use swear words, my friends at school would show me the naked photos from the "Foto Funnies" in *The National Lampoon* and I would turn my head away in embarrassment because I thought they were dirty, and I never made out with a girl until I was eighteen. What kind of geek is that to let into a fraternity? To top it off, every time I masturbated I thought I was going to hell.

I actually went to a mental health counselor at Kent State because of this masturbation problem. I wanted him to help me stop doing it. He sent me to see a Methodist minister who told me that he masturbated, his wife masturbated, and that it was okay with God if I masturbated, too. Three cheers for God.

Other than that, college was great. Thanks to the brothers of Delta Tau Delta, I learned about brotherhood, friendship, and group planning. I also got drunk, high, and laid for the first times in my life by the end of my freshman year. Unfortunately, I got drunk and high more than I got laid, and was academically dismissed a year later.

It's not that I was stupid and couldn't understand my classes, it's that I never went to the classes in the first place. I was too busy getting drunk and high, and trying to get laid.

I actually ended up being academically dismissed twice from Kent State, each time for pretty much the same reason. Then, after I did my first stand-up gig on *The Tonight Show*, I got a letter from the Kent State Alumni Association asking me for money. And after I got *The Drew Carey Show*, they had me in their homecoming parade.

So . . . hey, kids! Stay in school!

Another great influence in my life was the Marine Corps reserves. I was twenty-two and living in Mission Viejo, California, with my brother Neal when I joined. I had no job, hardly any clothes (everything I owned had been stolen from me a few months before in Las Vegas), and didn't want to bum off my brother anymore.

Joining the reserves appealed to me because I wasn't sure if I would like the military life, and I figured that way at least I'd only have to put up with it one weekend a month and two weeks during the summer. I originally wanted to join the navy reserves, but while I was looking at the brochures in the lobby of the recruiting office, the marine recruiter came out to the lobby and told me to stop by his office before I left.

It was an easy choice after that. The navy office was always cluttered and disorganized. The marine office was neat as a pin with every paper straightened on every single desk. One time, I walked in and caught one of the navy recruiters sleeping at his desk. The marines were always sitting up straight and ready to go. The army was never a real consideration, and besides, the army recruiter couldn't answer half my questions. The marines knew everything I wanted to know and the answers came quickly, without any bullshit.

The only hesitation that I had was that I was worried about all the beatings I'd heard about that take place in boot camp. The recruiter assured me that all that was a thing of the past in the Marine Corps, and he was right. You only wish they would beat you. Then at least it would be over with and you could get on with your training day.

But no. Instead it was fingertip push-ups until your arms collapsed, "mountain climbers" until you were ready to pass out, or sit-ups until you were ready to puke. Another favorite game was when they would have you rolling around in a dusty pit while the sweat poured off your face and made the dirt and sand stick to your face like a thousand annoying bugs. But they never hit you. That would've been too kind.

There were so many times, as the platoon went through their "punishment exercises," that I thought, "Just hit me, motherfucker. C'mon, I can take it. Right in the face. Hit me and get it over with. But holy shit, stop the push-ups!"

The things I learned in the Marine Corps have stayed with me to this day. I hate being late, I'm very organized, and I'm not afraid to take responsibility for my own actions, just to name a few. And, you could scream at me at the top of your lungs and call me all the names you want. It wouldn't even faze me.

As much as being in the Marine Corps reserves helped to turn me around and allow me to feel better about myself, books helped even more.

I sincerely believe that without the advice I've found in self-help books, I would not be the successful person that I am today. Or, the even more successful person I know that I'm going to be tomorrow.

These books have taught me to set goals, to believe in myself, to make an honest assessment of my abilities, how to stay focused on things that are important to me . . . so many good things that I can't list them all here.

Napoleon Hill, Dale Carnegie, W. Clement Stone, Og Mandino, Denis Waitley, Zig Ziglar, Brian Tracy, Dr. Wayne Dyer, Anthony Robbins, The Nightingale-Conant Company, and many others, all have influenced me more than anyone else in my life. Thank you, thank you, thank you.

And of course, there's my mother. She stood by me through all this, supporting me spiritually and financially, believing in me, and loving me. And I love her. More than words can say.

There's lots more to my life before I started doing stand-up and got on TV. I lived in Las Vegas off and on for a few years, worked as a bank teller and as a waiter, did some phone sales . . . but I've gone on too long already. That's pretty much it.

Maybe someday, when I'm old and *The Drew Carey Show* is as beloved as *Taxi* and is on *TV Land* every night in reruns, I'll fill you in on the details. Don't hold your breath. *Taxi* was too good a show for that to happen.

In the meantime, enjoy the photos. They're worth a thousand words apiece, you know.

Shaved and pierced. But I swear I'm not gay.

My dad (far left) standing by the bar at his lodge. I'm a chip off the old block.

My dad's last employee ID. He was dead less than a year later.

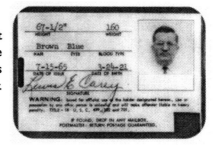

137

Age 7.

Age 9.

Age 12?
I can't remember.
It's all a blur.

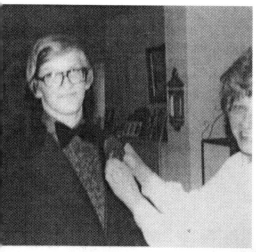

Prom night. That's
my mom on the right.

High School Graduation Day.
I'm not gay I tell ya! Ow!
Stop it! I told ya I'm not gay!

First year in college.

The real reason I tried to kill myself in college. Actually, this was for a contest that took place during Greek Week: "Miss Greek Week." Each fraternity "volunteered" one of its members to be dressed in drag by a sorority, and the cutest girl won. I won. That's my real hair. I'm not gay, honest.

Mr. Brute. Top row, far left.

The happiest marine.

From my old Marine Corps ID.
The best picture anyone's
ever taken of me.

In the marines. That's me
in the center. I'm not gay.
Really.

141

My first short-course biathlon.
I actually thought I was fat
in this picture.

In my kitchen in Cleveland.
I was a waiter at the Hilton
out on Rockside Road
back then.

My last Halloween costume. I dyed my
hair and went as "a guy with no pants."

142

STORIES OF
THE
UNREFINED

The first story I ever wrote, and the first thing that I wrote for this book, was the story *Mi Pelea* that starts out this section. Naturally, I was eager to show it to people to get their opinions on whether I had any chance at writing a book or not, and one of the first people to see it was my assistant, Marcy.

When I first wrote it, the title was *A True Story*, because it was, except for the ending, entirely true and based on my best memories of the incident. Everyone thought it was funny, which was a relief, even though the editors and publishers and my book agent all said, in their own polite way, that it was "too dark" and would scare off the average reader.

Heeding their advice, the next story I wrote was the even darker and more violent *A Friend In Need*. Unlike *Mi Pelea*, it was a total work of fiction. Once again, I showed it to Marcy to get her opinion.

She stood off in the corner of my home office, not laughing or even smiling much, even though I thought it was the funniest story of the two I had written.

"What's the matter?" I asked her. "Don't you like it?"

"Well, yeah, it's funny and everything," she said, searching for a way not to hurt my feelings. "I just worry about you personally, that's all."

I didn't say it at the time, but I thought, "Wow, even my good and trusted assistant Marcy is turned off by the dark tone of my story. Maybe some of the descriptions *are* too graphic."

The next day, I finally asked her to explain specifically what she meant when she said she "worried about me personally." She blurted out, "Well, dude, I mean . . . do you really want people to know all this stuff about you? All those things you did?" She looked helplessly down at the floor and shook her head. She didn't know that I had made the whole story up.

No wonder she was worried.

Now, to save anyone else from the confusion that poor Marcy had, let me assure you that this entire section is fiction.

Of course some of the stories, in whole or in part, are based on things that really happened to me and then were twisted into a work of fiction (like *Mi Pelea*). And, a lot of the characters are made up from a combination of people that I've actually known at one time or another.

So think of these stories as kind of a "Drew Carey In the Fourth Demension," as fictionalized as the guy on the television show. But, like the guy on the television show, still close enough to the real Drew to scare me.

If you want to get fancy and read them in the order they were written to see if I became a better writer as I went along, it goes *Mi Pelea*, then *A Friend in Need*, then *The Christmas Story*, *The Royal*, and *Tackling Jim Brown*. I started *Jim Brown* only four days before the deadline for the book, sweating it the entire time.

If you want to get real fancy and discuss the stories like you were in an English class: In *Tackling Jim Brown*, the character of Larry turned out to be a metaphor for the book, and reflects my feelings toward it at the time.

MI PELEA

I miss Cleveland in the winter. Not the bitter cold days when every breath threatens to shatter your lungs like a hammer taken to a pane of glass; but the crisp, clear days when you can hear the crunch of the snow under every step, and all the air around you seems clean and fresh. Like God made it that day just for you.

It was on one of those perfect winter days, a December 27th, when I walked into Kenny King's to get a little something to eat. The sun had just set, and it was crowded with people eating dinner after returning gifts to the Parmatown Mall. Families and old people mostly, which is why I liked it there.

Kenny King's was a pleasant and quiet place, unpretentious in every way, from the neutral-colored walls to the burgers and chicken menu. Home of the Double Big King, a gigantic, double-fisted cheesburger that dripped grease and love. A favorite of the working men and women of suburban Parma, Ohio.

Of course, I wasn't working much back then, but I had just spent a grueling hour and a half trying to figure out how to hang drywall in my basement and figured that Kenny King's was the best place to take my well-deserved break. A sassy waitress and a no-nonsense cup o' joe, that's what a hard-workin' man like me needs at the end of his day. That, and a beer, but I was on the wagon. I'd recently had a couple of embarrassing and dangerous episodes in my life because of my weakness for strong drink and loose women, and thought I'd take it easy for a while.

I lived within the Cleveland city limits, but barely. Parma started about two blocks away, and I used to walk over there all the time to eat, make fun of the people that lived there, and leave.

Parma is the city that we made fun of while everyone else in the country made fun of us. In Cleveland, we don't tell Polish jokes. We tell Parma jokes. ("How does a woman from Parma tease her hair? Nyah nyah nyah." Stupid jokes like that.) I think that the only reason God created Parma was so us sophisticates in Cleveland could mock it.

As much as my friends and I made fun of Parma while we were growing up, it still had a Kenny King's that was within walking distance, and the mall had a Gap, so I was over in Parma all the time.

The drywall was part of a Carey family project that started

when my father tried to turn our basement into a den/bed-room. He died before he could finish it and even though I was only twenty-four, I knew that I, too, would be dead before anything was ever finished down there, because I have as much talent for putting up two-by-fours and drywall as a dog has for singing opera. It is still not finished to this day. Regardless, it gave me something to do besides look for a job, and it let me fool my family into thinking that I was being productive.

Making everyone think that I had something going on with my life took up most of my days back then. You can't believe how much hard work it is to con people into thinking that you're productive and busy. Always thinking up things to tell them you're going to do tomorrow, having to exaggerate every minute of your nowhere day . . . it's worse than having a job. At least when you're employed, when people ask about your day you can tell them to shut up and mind their own business.

When you're a do-nothing twenty-four-year-old you need to always have a fresh line of bullshit ready to sling at the most innocent of questions. People would walk up to me on the street and say something like, "Hey Drew, nice weather, huh?"

"Well, yeah," I'd answer nervously, "but the car wash has all the guys they need on account of it's been so nice that they're using all their regulars, but the guy said to come back when it's raining and he'd try me. Hey, can you lend me five dollars? The fucking bank did something to my ATM card and now the thing won't take it. Ha ha ha! The shit just keeps rollin' down-hill, don't it? Ha ha ha!"

I didn't want anyone to see me that night, and I slinked over to the emptiest part of the counter. It wasn't because my clothes were covered with sweat, drywall dust, and cobwebs, but be-cause I was wearing my marine-issued geek glasses that I wore on my weekends in the reserves. I usually wore contacts back then because I was lean, athletic, and vain, but they had been bothering my eyes and so I went with the ugliest glasses on earth. Throughout the military, they are referred to as "birth-control glasses" because they are such thick, black monstrosities that they are a repellent to all but the loneliest and neediest of women.

I had just settled down with my Double Big King burger and a cup of coffee. Double Big Kings are great. I could taste every layer as my teeth ripped through it. Bun, then lettuce, quickly followed by just the right mix of mayonnaise, mustard, and ketchup. Just after that, the first bit of melted cheese and the first juicy grease of the burger. At the same time, my lower teeth were already past the lower layer of burger and cheese, and my tongue was busy sending heady flavor signals to the primitive, lizard part of my brain.

That was the love part of the Double Big King that I mentioned earlier. That undefinable moment of goodness that sent alpha shock waves of near-coital euphoria from your taste buds to your medulla and points beyond. A fairy-tale, only-in-romance-novels love.

If I speak in the tongues of men and of angels, but have not Double Big Kings, I am only a resounding gong or a clanging cymbal. For God so Double Big Kinged the world, that he gave his only begotten son. Double Big King your neighbor as you Double Big King yourself.

I don't know how long I had been sitting there. I used to have these kinds of food blackouts at Kenny King's all the time back then, where one minute I was taking the first heavenly bite out of my burger, and the next thing I knew it was a half-hour later and I was staring at an empty plate with no knowledge of what had happened in between. It was in the middle of one of these spells when they came in.

There were three of them, and they were loud, drunk, and oblivious: Two burly guys that looked like ex-high school linebackers and an old man I recognized as one of the regulars from Baron's, the bar next door. It was strictly a shot-and-beer joint. I worked there one summer and never even plugged in the blender. Once, a woman who was obviously lost came in and ordered a Manhattan. Me and the other bartender had to look it up.

Burly Number One was a big Irish-looking guy with curly blond hair down to his shoulders. He was dressed like a construction worker. Burly Number Two was an Italian-Greek mutt with short dark hair and a mustache that needed a trim. He was dressed like he borrowed money from the construction worker.

The Old Man was a pitiful old geezer who I had never seen sober. During the summer I worked the morning shift at Baron's, he used to be already staggering when he slumped onto his regular barstool and ordered a shot of the lower-shelf whiskey and fishbowl draft of Labbatt's. The bill for this deadly combo came to a dollar fifty. He would tip me a dime.

The two big guys had to hold him up as they stumbled to the counter. I stared straight down at my half-eaten dinner, mumbling "Awww fuck" under my breath as they sat down next to me. The half of me that had already eaten thought that maybe they would just eat quickly and then leave, but the still-hungry half of me knew better.

They each ordered fried chicken and snorted and slurped through their meal, loudly smacking their lips and wiping their mouths on their sleeves. They belched as often as they breathed out. French fries were dipped into the communal glass ketchup container while they made loud comments about how nice the waitress's ass was (it wasn't). One recounted a humorous anecdote about a "Polack, a nigger, and a Jew" trapped on an island together. I didn't quite catch the ending, but it brought a half-chewed-chicken explosion of guffaws from his countermates.

While the last of the bones were being sent clinking onto the cheap china plates, the blond guy decided to order a five-piece chicken dinner to go. "I promised the old lady I'd get her and the kids something," he slurred.

I was kind of glancing at them out of the corner of my eye because I could see that they would be leaving soon, and I would finally be able to enjoy a quiet cup of coffee without being jostled or being forced to listen to another nigger joke. As the blond guy took his to-go box of chicken under his arm and got up, he winked at the old man and, smiling, shoved the check for it into his flannel jacket.

Now, a five-piece order of The Colonel's Original Recipe Kentucky Fried Chicken from Kenny King's only costs about five bucks, including corn, slaw, and tax. Kenny King's owns about a dozen restaurants throughout Cuyahoga County and could easily afford to lose five dollars. But, you let one guy do it, and then pretty soon another guy does it, and the next thing you know, you have societal breakdown and anarchy on your hands. I believed that then, and I believe that now. No matter how it turned out, I know that what I did, I did for America.

Blondie had already stumbled out while Black Hair and the old man stood at the register and paid the check for the dinners that they had already eaten. They were almost halfway out the door by the time I motioned the waitress with the nice ass that really wasn't over and told her what had happened, and while she ran out into the cold to catch up to Blondie, I hustled quickly over to the other two before they could leave the building.

"Hey," I said to the old man, tapping him on the shoulder,

"your friend's gonna have to come back and pay for his check."
He turned and looked up at me like a drunk fish.

"What check?" he mumbled stupidly. His eyes crossed and
recrossed again, trying desperately to get in sync with each
other but failing.

"C'mon, man, I know you. From Baron's. I saw him take
the check with him." I tried to be as reasonable and firm as I
could manage.

Black Hair said, "What the fuck you talkin' about . . ." but
the old man was already reaching for his wallet and heading
back to the register.

"All right, all right," he said, giggling at the fact that they
had gotten caught. I was relieved to see that that was all there
was going to be to it. The old man would pay the five dollars
for the chicken and that would be that.

I followed them back to the register, and just as the money
was coming out of the old man's wallet, the front door flew
open and Blondie came roaring back in with the waitress right
behind him. "What the fuck!" he yelled. "I didn't take no
fucking check! What the fuck is this?!"

"Hey man," I turned to him, forgetting how stupid I looked
in my crew cut and thick glasses, covered with bits of drywall
that I had ruined just hours ago. "I saw you take the check and
put it in your pocket."

"What are you? A fucking cop? I'll knock your glasses right
off your fucking face!"

"Oh yeah?" I said defiantly, removing my specs. "I'll take
my glasses off . . ."

And that was all it took. A lifetime of carefully avoiding any
type of physical confrontation whatsoever gone right down the
drain.

I wasn't afraid, mind you. Since joining the marines, I've

never been afraid of a fight, but I knew from witnessing enough of them how needless and dangerous they usually are. Real street fights are scary to watch, and I've always depended on my quick wit and friendly manner to get me out of any potentially dangerous situation. The trick, though, is remembering to be friendly and quick-witted. Either that, or intimidating and loud. At the moment though, I was small, quiet, unfriendly, and dull.

As I set my glasses down near the register, he charged at me, getting me in a bear hug and pushing me backward along the counter. "Motherfucker! Fucking fat-ass cocksucker fuck! Arrr-gggggghhh!" we yelled at each other.

We flew into a metal bus cart, sending dirty dishes and dirtier water flying everywhere, and landed with me flat on my stomach and him on top of me. I quickly curled into a protective ball on my hands and knees (a move I perfected as the worst wrestler in the history of James Ford Rhodes High School) just as his big, meaty hands covered my face and tried to gouge at my eyes.

Believe it or not, right then some guy in the booth next to us yelled, "Hey now! Take that outside!" like I had a choice of where to get my ass kicked.

Now, evidently, Blondie was much drunker than Dark Hair, because up to this point, he hadn't even thrown a punch. He was just basically wrestling with me and trying to gouge my eyes out. When Dark Hair ran over to the toppled bus cart to give Blondie a hand, I saw two of the cooks jump on top of him and he shook them off like they were old overcoats. Dark Hair didn't seem to be drunk at all at that point, and as pissed off as a bear that had lost his picnic basket.

I saw this while I was grabbing Blondie's wrist and pulling his hand down. I remember thinking something like, "Holy fuck!" when I saw what Dark Hair did to the cooks, and then

I bit into Blondie's middle finger as hard as I could without breaking the skin.

He yelped and jumped up enough for me to spring out from under him and turn around. "C'mon, you fat fucking fuck, ya!" I threatened. "Fuck you, motherfucking fuck!" he retorted, and ran at me again, hugging me low around my waist and hurling me between two stools, slamming my back into the counter. My arms were flailing, and every dish on the counter went crashing to the floor. I noticed a line of people scurrying quickly out the front door.

Because of how Blondie had wrapped himself around me, I was able to easily reach down with my right arm and get him in a solid headlock. But he was too big and strong for me to move anywhere, so I just jumped up and down and slammed his head into the edge of the counter until Black Hair jumped up on the stool next to us and punched me in the face.

This startled me. Like I said, I had never been in a real fight before this, and even though it was only a glancing blow and didn't hurt at all, it made me stop and loosen up on Blondie enough for him to pop his head up and glare at me and catch his breath.

We stared at each other for just a half a second, and then I punched him twice in the face and came out from between the stools, carefully keeping the big drunk lummox between me and his sober-fighting friend.

"Fuck you!" One of us yelled.

"Cocksucking pussy!"

"C'mon and get me, you fat fuck!"

"Fuck you, fat ass!"

I was quickly running out of clever ways to use the word *fuck*, and was relieved to see five Parma policemen coming through the door. There's usually not much going on in Parma, which is why so many of them were available so soon.

Dark Hair was sober enough to be apologetic and humble, and smart enough to call the cops "sir" whenever he said anything to them. They let him go.

Blondie was arrested for whatever they charge you with when you get into a drunken fight over five dollars' worth of chicken. The old man was arrested for being a stupid old drunk.

The concerned citizen that wanted us to take our fight outside came over, red-faced with rage, to where the one cop was talking to me, pointing his finger and yelling, "These two were using bad words in front of my kids!" The cop rolled his eyes and waved him off.

But the cop didn't even make notes as I told him my side of the story, choosing instead to stare dully at me like I was some kind of dumb ass for getting into a fight over five dollars' worth of chicken that didn't even belong to me in the first place. I tried to explain my theory of societal breakdown to him, but he wasn't buying it. I think he didn't arrest me only because he felt sorry for me.

We had broken well over five dollars worth of plates and other things, as well as driving out almost every diner that had crowded the restaurant just minutes ago, and the manager ended up paying for everyone's meal which added up to several hundred dollars in lost revenue. The waitresses lost tip money. I was covered in cold, spilled coffee and mustard, and my left pant leg was caked with sticky old chocolate milkshake from when we were lying in the ruins of the bus cart.

All in all, I thought that it was a pretty successful crime-fighting night. I saved the honor of Kenny King's, fought off two big drunks, getting in a bite and two punches to the face, and I didn't have a scratch on me. My first fight! Wooooo! I was the King of the World! You never got me down, Ray!

★　★　★

When I got home, I had a reaction to being in my first big fight that I never would've expected: surviving primitive combat had made me the horniest man alive. My penis felt brand new and never bigger, a wide-eyed youth eager to take on every woman, man, and Rodmanesque in-betweener in the world. I could've fucked thin air.

No wonder old boxers never want to retire.

Now, if I had a job and a future and didn't spend every day thinking of excuses for the next day, I might have had a girl-friend to share my excitement with. But for some reason, chicks hate losers, so I did the laundry by hand.

I had to put the washer through three loads before I could relax enough to go to sleep. Three times in one hour! A personal best record that still stands to this day. But the thing is, even though I masturbated quite a bit in those days, I never did it three times in an hour before, which is why I think my elbow went out on me. It hurt like hell, too. Just as I was starting my third round of spasms, I felt a sharp pain shoot through my right elbow and paralyze me.

If you want to know exactly how it felt, the next time you're masturbating, just as you first start to have your orgasm, stab yourself.

I gingerly rolled out of bed, holding my elbow and squinting in the dark without my glasses, trying to make it down the hall to the bathroom so I could see if it was swollen or not and clean up. Because of the blinding pain in my arm, I didn't pay much attention to the fact that my underwear was still bunched around my ankles, forcing me to take dangerous little baby steps down the hall.

When I got to the middle of the hallway, where the top of the stairway was, I put my left hand out to steady myself against the corner, allowing my right arm to dangle disagreeably for just a moment while I caught my breath. It really hurt, no shit, and the pain was making me start to sweat like a cold Pepsi bottle on a hot summer day.

My left hand was so coated with perspiration (that's my story and I'm sticking to it) that as I reached out to grab the corner of the wall and the stairwell, it slipped out from under me and I went tumbling down the stairs like a spastic Hollywood stunt man. Face, bad elbow, good elbow, face, face, shoulder, lower spine, right ankle, and face. I'm surprised my balls didn't somehow find a way to bash themselves into the banister while I was at it.

I had to wear a neck brace for six weeks, have my arm in a sling for a month, and use a crutch to walk. This is not to mention the accompanying bruises and abrasions, and the fact that while I healed, I couldn't masturbate at all because of the pain. It was as if someone had shot my horse after it won the Kentucky Derby.

The hardest part of the night was trying to clean up and get dressed to drive myself to the emergency room. I felt like one of those farm boys that you hear about every once in a while who get their arms cut off in a hay combine and have to dial 911 with their nose. I really should've just called an ambulance, but I was too embarrassed by the whole thing to let them see how it happened.

When I finally got to Deaconess Hospital, I fell exhausted and crying from my car onto the cement driveway, unable to go any farther. Blood flowed from a gash above my eye. I was missing a shoe.

Interns and nurses rushed to my side, and as I was being wheeled into the ER on a gurney, I looked up into the face of the blondest, most attractive nurse that I had ever seen in my life. Blue, wading-pool eyes, skin that glowed like the halo of an angel, and huge tits. She looked like she paid her way through nursing school by being a supermodel.

She took my hand and gently brushed a tear from my face. "Oh my God, what happened to you?" she purred.

Oh God, her voice. The way her lips moved . . . so soft . . . so full and perfect . . .

I swallowed hard, taking in the entire measure of her beauty, and managed to get one more tear to roll out pitifully from my bloodshot eye. "I got into a fight at Kenny King's," I sobbed.

THE
CHRISTMAS
STORY

Let me start out right off the bat and tell you that I don't like Christmas at all. Hate it, in fact.

It's greedy, crowded, and overhyped. It brings out the worst kind of sanctimonious behavior in everyone that participates in it. People try to make up for a year's worth of indifference with one good deed, and then they shove it back in our faces like a politician who needs a vote. "Oh, I'm so good and holy! Look at all the good things I did this Christmas!"

All the songs are bad. It wastes electricity. All the people who don't drive very well go out shopping at the same time and wind up right in front of me when I'm in a hurry. It alienates Jews and Muslims. All the clothes in the Gap get thrown around so you can't find your size right away. I just wish it would go away.

There are more suicides during the Christmas season than any other time of year. Especially in Sweden.

There are lots of reasons that I don't care for this annual exercise in hypocrisy, but I couldn't explain it all to my mother right now. It was cold in the desert at night, and I was at a pay phone without many quarters, so I had to make it quick. After the initial pleasantries, letting her know that yes, I was fine here in Las Vegas, and no, I hadn't been gambling much (I had), I broke the news.

"Hey Mom, listen. Um, I don't . . . I don't want you to get me anything for Christmas this year." I looked down at my feet, afraid to meet her eyes, even though she was over a thousand miles away.

"What?" She said it like the line had gone dead. I glanced at the shelf below the phone. Only three quarters left.

"Yeah, I'm not going to do Christmas this year. I mean, I'm getting out of it."

"What are you talking about? Is it money?"

"No, Mom, it's not money." Then quickly, "I just don't like Christmas anymore and I decided that I don't want to give any-body anything and I don't want anyone to give anything to me. So, I don't want anyone to send me any cards or anything. And I won't get anything for anyone else. Okay?"

"What's happened? What's wrong?"

"Nothing. I just don't like it anymore."

"Well, I don't know what to say . . ." Maybe she thought I was sick.

"Look, I don't . . . it's, I just don't want to do it anymore. Would you let Aunt Alta and everyone know? Save me some calls? Tell them I don't want anything."

"Well, all right, if that's what you want."

"Right. I don't want anything."

I told her the real reason I dropped out of the most beloved holiday in the world a year or so later, after I had one miserable failure after another in Las Vegas and had to move back to Cleveland. I seems like I have to tell everyone every year.

You see, I had gotten my own kind of religion for a while that year back in Vegas, and while reading through various church pamphlets and my own Bible, I discovered that Christmas is not a religious holiday at all. Go ahead and look it up if you want to. Christmas is not in the Bible.

What *is* in the Bible is what's popularly known as "The Christmas Story"; the birth of Jesus in Bethlehem. But that's it. It never says to go out and celebrate his birth by putting up trees and lights and sending each other gifts. In fact, there's a verse in Deuteronomy that says *not* to put up a tree like the pagans do. Further, all through the Bible it gives strict instructions to *not* adopt any pagan holidays or customs at all. So I don't. And, for the record, neither did Jesus.

Jesus never put up a tree and exchanged gifts, or left cookies out for Santa. He never made a harried, last-minute trip to the mall, or spent Christmas Eve night cursing at a toy that he couldn't put together. He celebrated Passover. So, if you want to be more like Jesus, pass the matzo.

Quick! How many wise men were there?

Who knows? The Bible never says how many there were. It says that there were just "wise men."

Quick! When was Jesus born?

Well, we know for sure that it *wasn't* on December 25th. That's a pagan holiday. It was popular in ancient Roman days when Constantine of Rome wanted to reunite the city, and declared that from then on, they were all Christians. And, to help celebrate the new state religion, we're reassigning the Sun-God holiday that you love so much, and all its customs, to the celebration of the birth of Jesus Christ. You can still keep all of your pagan traditions, we're just going to call them something else.

Jesus was born all right, but he wasn't born on December 25th. I know because it says so in the Bible. He was born while the "shepherds watched their flocks by night," which was probably no later than October. Shepherds have their flocks penned up during cold winter months like December. We don't know when he was born, really.

During the first few years of being a Christmas dropout, my mother always got me "just a little present," just to make herself happy, but I never returned the courtesy.

"Mom, I don't want anything."

"Oh," she'd smile, playfully slapping me on the arm, "it's just a stocking. You can get a stocking from your own mother, can't you?" She'd jump up and hand me down the well-worn red "sock" that she got from Halle's department store when I was a kid, with "Drew" written out across it in flaking gold glitter-script.

Before she remarried and moved out of the house, it hung on a cheap cardboard imitation fireplace that we set up along the wall near the stairway. It had a red Christmas tree bulb for a fire, and a slotted aluminum disk would spin above it to make the "fire" crackle. She had a real fireplace now that she was married to George, but it didn't work. It came with a real mantel, though, and there hung the Carey boys' stockings every year. Whether one of them liked it or not.

"Here," she'd say, handing me the stocking as if it were an afterthought. "It's just a few things I found at Marc's I thought you could use." AA batteries. A Rubik's Cube. A mini flashlight/lighter combination that took AAA batteries. A pocket atlas. Some cookies. A giant popcorn ball.

She'd also wrap up some athletic socks or T-shirts for me and put them under the tree. As long as they were in a small box and didn't cost much, I guess she never felt she was *really* giving me a proper Christmas present so she wasn't *really* going against my wishes.

One year, around Halloween (another pagan holiday that I avoid), my mother came to me for a favor.

You see, every year, our entire family got together at someone's house on Christmas Eve (lately, at my cousin Carol's) and exchanged gifts. And, ever since I can remember, someone played Santa.

When I was growing up it was always Uncle Tom or Uncle George. Then, other relatives took over. My cousin Danny, Carol's husband Jim, somebody *always* did it. Now, for some strange reason she wanted it to be my turn.

"Since you don't have anything to do with Christmas," she said uncomfortably, "I was wondering if you would play Santa this year for the kids."

Huh? It was like walking up to a fat rabbi and saying, "Hey, you've got a beard. Hows about playing Santa at our church?"

"Aw, Mom. I don't think—"

"I've got it almost done," she said, pulling the evil red suit from a box by her chair. "See? I bought some boots at Pay-Less that are your size, and this belt should just fit . . ."

She convinced me that I wouldn't really be violating my beliefs, that I would just be helping the family out. They weren't presents from me, after all, they were from other people. To other people. I was just the . . . facilitator. It was that same melodic, sweet-talking voice she used to use to get me to eat my peas when I was three.

"Brian, what am I gonna do?" I sank lower into the booth. We were at Kenny King's, a local coffee shop that specialized in hot coffee and cold reality. There was also a Denny's nearby, but I worked waiting tables at a Denny's and couldn't stand to be in one once I punched out.

"Hey man," Brian put up his hands and laughed. "Leave me out of it." Brian was slim and dark-haired. We met in fourth grade when we sat next to each other in the trumpet section of our grade school's orchestra. We'd sat next to each other in every school band and orchestra since.

It was great to be out of school for so long and still have friends from there. We were constantly calling each other with the latest record we heard, trying to out-do each other in finding the coolest unknown groups.

Brian always out-cooled me in that respect because he worked in a record store and heard all the latest stuff before anyone else. He also worked weekends playing horn in a polka band that traveled throughout northeast Ohio and western Pennsylvania, so his musician friends (who also worked in record stores) gave him a lot of tips on the latest sounds, too.

If I heard a good joke somewhere, I told it to Brian first. If there was something good on TV, Brian called me first to tell me to turn it on. If there was a good movie out, we saw it together. He was, and remains still, one of my closest and dearest friends.

"Hey, I have an idea," I said to my friend, as if just thinking of it. I had been rehearsing this moment for hours, starting right before I'd asked him to meet me here. "Why don't *you* do it?"

I waited a beat, like I was just then thinking it through. "Yeah!" I laughed. "You in the Santa suit! It'll be great! Oh, man, what a *great* gag! My mom won't know what happened when she sees me walk in with you!" I grinned like an idiot, hoping inside that I wasn't overselling it. I'd talked Brian into doing stuff he didn't want to do lots of times before, and I knew that I had to present it just right.

"Naw, man. I mean, that's just between you and your family. I don't want to get in the middle of all that."

"Aw, c'mon."

Silence.

"*C'mon.*"

More silence. I looked at him for a full beat.

"Naw, c'mon, man. Just do it. Just this once. It'll be great and you'll really be doing me a favor. C'mon."

I was from the school of thought that if you used the same word often enough, it would take on magic powers and change the mind of the person that you were trying to persuade. The three words that you can use for this are "c'mon," "please," and "stop." There are really no other words that even remotely come close to fitting the "say and repeat" rule.

"No," he said finally. "No, no, no."

Just try and run a simple errand during the week before Christmas in Cleveland. Just try.

I really needed to jam my way down Ridge Road and get to Parmatown Mall. Parmatown Mall was the home of Antonio's Pizza, the best pizza in the city. They had a full-service restaurant outside the mall, and a by-the-slice outlet in the food court. I was jonesing for some Antonio's really bad, and wanted to get a couple of slices before I took my nap and headed to my third-shift job at Denny's.

Usually, it was a fifteen-minute drive at night, twenty minutes tops. But now the streets were too full of Christmas shopping idiots and it was like driving through mud on a tricycle. Solid citizens in Volvos and minivans who were driving the *speed limit* (Can you believe it! *The speed limit!*) like they expected some kind of prize for obeying the "law." So, what should've been a fifteen-minute drive took me a whole thirty-five minutes, which I knew was going to eat into my nap time. Yeah thanks, brownnoser. Thanks for slowing me up and ruining my day. Here's your gold star.

When I finally got to the mall it was bedlam. It took me a good ten minutes just to find a parking spot, dodging pea-brained shoppers who wouldn't walk to the side of the parking lanes, but had to meander down the middle. And then, I had to park at the very back of the lot and hoof it through the freezing snow to the mall's entrance.

Inside the mall was like the end of the world. Gangs of rude teenagers with big hair stood in gaggles blocking any reasonable adult (like me) who knew where they were going and why. Doddering old people walked as *sllllllooooooow* as they could, making it impossible for me to get around them without knocking someone else over. Screaming children ran unsupervised from one end of the mall to the other.

And Jesus, wouldn't you know it? The line at Antonio's stretched all the way down to Orange Julius, almost making it to the pretzel stand. And to top it off, the pizza line was full of the type of amateurs that only come out of their houses in December to shop and cause trouble.

"What kind of pizza do you have?" they would ask, after standing in line for twenty minutes in front of the big, electronic menu. What kind of pizza do you think they have at the stupid *mall*, you idiots? Goat cheese and shrimp, with a balsamic

vinaigrette? They have PEPPERONI, CHEESE, and SAU-
SAGE, like everybody else in the world!!! What do they have
to drink? Coke! Pepsi! 7Up! You know, the most popular soft
drinks available! The ones that you should know by heart if
you're any kind of American! You're a moron! Get out of the
line and never leave your house again! Die! Die! Die!

Let's just hope these people don't vote, or have children.
(Oh, I know they do. I just hope they don't.)

Of course, there was no line at the Golden Pagoda ("The
Freshest Sushi In Parma!"), but nothing was going to make me
or anyone else that shopped at Parmatown start experimenting
with food.

Maybe if I had gotten here sooner the line wouldn't have
been as long, but thanks to my mother, now I'll never know.

She had me standing on a kitchen chair doing alterations on
the Santa suit for almost an hour that afternoon, with nothing
to do but watch a tape she and her husband George made of a
Phil Donahue Show that originally aired back in July.

Ever since George got his first VCR, he and my mother had
stopped watching regularly scheduled television like the rest of
us and taped everything for later viewing. He had three VCRs
going all the time and bought blank video tapes by the box
full. He also had a high-end Korean camcorder and the newest
Japanese TV.

And yet, despite the lack of convenience, they still used a
rotary dial phone because George didn't want to spend the extra
two dollars a month or whatever it was to the phone company.
I worried about them in an emergency. I mean, how do you
dial the police on a rotary dial phone?

Nine.

One.

One.

Even though the fitting seemed to take forever, I had to admit that my mother had outdone herself. She'd made a lot of clothes in her lifetime, but this was really something.

It was a masterpiece of tailoring and Santa-suit design. She had spent countless hours on it, working her aging, arthritic fingers to the point of numbness, creating the best Santa suit that I, or anyone else, had ever seen.

"Well, glad to see your mother is almost done with that darn suit," George chuckled, changing a tape in VCR number three. "That's all she's been doing. We haven't even wrapped presents yet and I haven't had a decent dinner in a month." He laughed like he was joking, but I knew that he wasn't. When she was finally through measuring and poking at me, she had me stand in front of a mirror so I could see how it looked. It wasn't quite finished, filled with pins and chalk marks, but it fit me perfectly. Shiny, black Santa boots, expensive (for us) red velour pants and jacket with real faux-fur trim. And a wide genuine leather belt to hold the pillow in. (I had no beer gut back in those days.) It was topped off with a state-of-the-art flowing white beard and hair, complete with fake white bushy eyebrows, and a jaunty Santa hat.

I was the embodiment of evil.

"Looks great, Mom. Ho ho ho," I said, tearing it off as fast as I could.

I picked it up from my mom's house, fully tailored, on December 23rd without trying it on again. I have yet to wear it, to this day.

★ ★ ★

My second cousin Danielle was the first one to see me when she answered the door at Carol's house.

"Oh, hi . . . Drew?" Danielle looked at me like she couldn't believe the getup I was wearing. Apparently, everyone in the house over the age of twelve knew that good old Uncle/Cousin Drew was going to be Santa Claus this year. "What happened?"

I was dressed casually, no tie, in the nicest clothes that I owned at the time. Black knit slacks, tan sweater, and my best pair of running shoes.

"Oh," I said breezily, rushing by her and taking off my parka, "I decided not to do it."

Carol and her daughter Missy were the next ones to see me. "You did *what?*" Carol exclaimed.

"Oh man, does your mom know?" Missy asked, looking quickly around the room to see if my mother was in sight.

"No," I said, smiling brightly, "Didn't tell her."

My mom didn't say anything at first when she first saw me walk into the den. She was sitting by herself, in one of Carol's expensive armchairs, contentedly watching the family come and go. She was probably thinking good Grandma thoughts about how proud she was of everyone and how much we all had grown. Then she saw me. Black slacks and a tan sweater.

I guess I hadn't really thought it out all the way through, because I never reckoned on how she would react when she first saw me without her Santa suit.

First, her eyes widened a little as they took me in, not quite registering the sight, or believing it. Then she sat up suddenly like I had slapped her across the face, her mouth dropping open and her hands gripping the arms of her chair all at once.

I walked over to her as casually as I could, but inside I was melting. My legs had gone rubbery, and my gut was being tied into a Gordian knot. Everyone knew how hard Mom had worked on that Santa suit. Everyone. And they all expected *somebody* in the family to be Santa, and she had promised to take care of it. *Promised.* To the whole family.

Some of the other relatives were looking at us, and my mother was trying hard not to let them see her break down. I watched her eyes well with tears. The same eyes that looked at mine with strength and love, soothing me after my father died when I was eight. The same eyes that sparkled with pride at every band recital, every school art project that hung on the refrigerator, every bad report card, every small victory I'd ever had in my life. The eyes that watched over me as I grew from a child into a man.

They were crying now. Crying and ashamed.

"Hi Mom." I could barely get the words out. She never looked at me. She stared straight ahead, trying to muster all the dignity she had left in her sixty-eight-year-old body. Her lips trembled as she spoke.

"If you didn't want to do it, you just should've said so. You just should've *told me*, before I went to *all that trouble.*" Her voice was cracked and broken.

"I'm sorry, Mom," I whispered. They were all staring now. "I just forgot."

"Oh, don't give me that!" she spat. "After all that *work.* Oh, I should've *known.*" She looked away from me, hiding her face in her hand.

She should've known. Now it was my turn to try not to cry. Another letdown from her baby boy, Drew. Presbyterian truant. College dropout. Las Vegas failure. Denny's employee.

The boy who ruined Christmas.

I looked at my watch. "Where the hell is Brian already?" I screamed to myself. "It's *been* five minutes, hurry your ass up."

He made a great entrance. Didn't even knock. He just swung the door open and let out a giant "Ho Ho Ho!" as he stomped the snow away from his thick leather boots. That was the only thing that didn't fit Brian. The boots. His feet were just a half-size bigger than mine, so I had given him money to get a pair of his own.

But everything else was just like Mom made it. The big bag of presents that I had given him before we left my house, the suit, the belt, the beard, the white eyebrows. . . . It was great.

I let out a giant breath of relief, and finally was able to look my mother in the face again. She was trembling, her tears flowing more freely than before, only now they ran past her beautiful, loving smile.

"Oh," she said, blinking back her tears. "Oh, I get it now. Oh, God . . ." I knelt down to hug her. She gripped me around my neck, and held me tightly, and with as much love as if I was newborn.

We held each other, loving mother and devoted son, for a full minute before she asked, "So who is it? Who did you get?"

"I'm not telling you," I smiled. "That's part of the prank."

And I didn't tell, either. Everyone wanted to know, of course. I wish I had a nickel for every time one of my relatives said, "Oh, c'mon," (there's that word again), "you can tell *me.*" But I just kept my trap shut.

"You'll never figure it out, you filthy pagans," I thought, smiling to myself as I surveyed the commotion in the living room.

The kids were ga-ga over their gifts, throwing paper and ribbon everywhere. "Thank you, Gramma B.!" "Thank you, Aunt Alta!" There were no "Thank you, Drews," but that was fine by me. The best thing about dropping out of Christmas is that it saves you a ton of money from not buying any gifts for people you see only once or twice a year.

"Santa" looked like he was having the time of his life, too, passing out presents like Rockefeller with a pocketful of dimes. A little too heavy on the "ho ho hos" if you ask me, but hey. It's only once a year, so live it up.

I was in the dining room grabbing another slab of pound cake when I heard the door open and all the kids yelling, " 'Bye, Santa! 'Bye!"

I wanted to thank Brian for the great job he did, and tell him where to leave the suit when he was done. Turning quickly, I shoved the cake into my mouth as I ran, and just missed him going out the door. No time to put on my shoes, I hurried outside in my stocking feet, down the porch steps into the freshly fallen snow, just in time to see him running around the side of the house toward the backyard.

"Hey, Brian!" I yelled. "Hey!"

"Yeah I know, I'm sorry," Brian said, coming up the front walk. Same red bag, same red suit and belt, same beard and hair. Crappier boots. "My car wouldn't start and I didn't know the number here to call ya."

I sent him home before anyone could see him, taking the bag of toys.

I went inside and passed them out myself.

A FRIEND IN NEED

The door was unlocked. Again. One more thing I've tried to be nice about, but of course, Larry didn't care.

The kitchen counter was so filthy that I was afraid to set my keys down on it. Empty beer cans and liquor bottles, some kind of liquid that had turned to crust, and, oh Jesus Christ. Cigarette butts! He put them out right on my counter! The counter that I eat off of! The counter that I used to eat off of. The counter that I'll never eat off of again. There was a note: "Drew, Need more cereal. Larry."

My jaw clenched tight as I entered the living room and my head started to twitch at the neck. Both actions were purely involuntary. I was probably grinding my teeth at night, too, but who cared anymore. That was a small problem now.

Dirty clothes on the living room floor. Again. Stale cigarette air. Again. Plus other, nonspecific odors that tended to accumulate when the doors and windows were always shut. Again. Living with Larry was like having five cats in the house. You could never hide the smell.

After a quick trip to the basement to drop off my supplies, I made my way upstairs to the only bathroom in my house. Separate bathrooms would have made things a lot easier, but this house ws so small I might as well have wished for the moon.

I was hoping the bathroom would be as I left it, knowing that it wouldn't be. It was awful. Larry, Larry, everywhere. Towels akimbo, toothpaste cap off, tube squeezed from the middle. His toothbrush sitting in a puddle on the counter. I reminded myself never to kiss him.

I had to lift the lid to the toilet with my foot like I was in a some backwoods roadside gas station, except that those places were cleaner. And they didn't have the hair that this place had. Dozens of little strands of hair, varying in thickness and length, had settled in blasphemously around the once-pristine tile floor.

It was all Larry's hair, I saw. I knew it so well by now. God, he was a gorilla. The simple act of rubbing a towel over his back after a shower left the room looking like an unswept barber shop. Some of it could've been mine. It had been falling out in clumps for the last three weeks, after all. Natalie's doing more than Larry's, maybe, but it was too late for that kind of thinking now.

I had also developed a stutter, which caused no small amount of concern at Bully's, where I was employed as a Professional Food Server. That's a waiter to those of you who never go out.

Bully's was, despite its name, a snooty, expensive place to eat. And it had a real caste system for its waiters based on (in order) how brown your nose was, how gay you were, and how good you looked. I struck out swinging on the first one (every kiss-ass attempt I made looked awkward), walked on the second one (welcoming and enjoying all things "gay" save for any actual sex acts themselves), and only hit a broken-bat single on the third one.

"I'm t-t-terribly s-sorry about the delay," I would start in, Larry's fat, stupid face flashing before me. He was, after all, the cause of everything bad in my life lately. "The k-kitchen's very busy tonight. M-may I b-b-buy you a drink, on th-the house?" What I wanted to say was, "Would you please remove your trousers so I can shove your pasta up your ass one strand at a time?" Fortunately, it wasn't constant, only rearing it's u-u-ugly head when things weren't going as sm-sm-smoothly as they should. But all it took was one table gone wrong, and I was off to stuttersville until well after the offenders paid their bill and left.

Ronald (no one ever dared call him Ron) was the general manager of Bully's and was such a stuck-up queen that all the gay guys called him Miss Liberace behind his back. And he wasn't as sympathetic to speech impediments as you would expect a man who lisps so much would be.

He used my stuttering as his excuse to screw me via the weekly schedule, cutting my income by over a third. Suddenly I was working more lunch shifts and less dinner shifts, always assigned to the crummiest, least-profitable section available.

The section I had been constantly banished to for the last two weeks was aptly named "the lows," because it was the only seating in the restaurant that wasn't elevated or near a window. It was instead located around the raw bar where the oysters and crab legs were kept on ice, and the main aisleway through the dining room. If the fishy smell didn't distract you from enjoying your expensive meal to the fullest, then the constant flow of waiters, waitresses, busboys, and customers being seated and going back and forth to the bathrooms would. No one ever made money in the lows.

The best money was in section two, just a few steps up from the main floor and surrounded by a railing which gave its diners a definite sense of privacy and exclusivity that the losers in the lows would never know. Just being there made them want to tip more. It was always packed with deal-making fat cats and couples on hot dates.

The lows always had people who had never eaten in an expensive restaurant before and couldn't believe that we charged six dollars for soup.

After I had used the toilet, I turned on the faucet with my elbows and washed my hands, drying them on my shirt. It was a technique I'd been forced to perfect over the last four weeks, and it still comes in handy at freeway rest stops.

Then it was back to the basement to get everything in order. I had a lot of preparing to do between now and when the bars closed.

Moving some boxes, I came across one I didn't recognize. It was Larry's, packed with mementos from his high school career, including our yearbook, his letterman's jacket, and Larry's diploma.

High school was the best time in Larry's life. He wrestled 156, and his teenage zenith was being fourth runner-up in the conference tournament in his senior year. Girls went crazy for him after that, finally noticing his tight wrestler's body and the soft layer of hair that covered his broad teenage chest like a

welcome mat. His large nose and bad teeth they suddenly ignored.

Teachers had always liked him even before he was a sports
hero. He was one of those kids who could walk the halls freely,
never asked for a pass or where he was going. Good old Larry.
Homecoming Court Alternate. Pep Club Advisory Committee.
He even played third trombone in the marching band.

Before he moved in with me, you could still go over to his
parents' house and find him strutting around with his shirt off
as if nothing had changed. He was now pot-bellied and balding,
with chest muscles that had turned into tits, but he didn't seem
to notice. And the lightly hairy chest that impressed the girls so
much in high school had spread like Kudzu. His upper arms,
shoulders, and back were all infested with it. Once, when we
were at the beach out in Sandusky, I noticed a group of high
school girls laughing at how gross his hairy body was. And they
weren't half as pretty as the girls that used to climb over themselves to be with him when he was their age.

I could've had a long honest talk with him about his keen
sense of denial but I never brought it up. It wouldn't have been
a good beer-buddy thing to do.

You see, that's all Larry ever was to me. A beer buddy. Even
in high school when we couldn't drink. He was a guy to tell
jokes with, see a movie, shoot the shit. He never came to me
with a problem, and I never came to him. We were so superfi-
cial and breezy with each other that it was almost the perfect
friendship.

The joke that got him fired from the auto plant went like
this: What does a tightrope walker and a guy getting a blow job
from Whoopi Goldberg have in common? They're both too
afraid to look down.

Larry told it all over the plant, and got big laughs all around.

Even from the women, who loved a good blow-job joke as much as any of the guys. All except for that one, that is. And nowadays, that's all it takes. Ten years of steady employment down the drain. Pack up your nudie pen and your wind-up hopping penis and get out.

"Sexual harassment! Can you believe it! I was telling a joke!" Larry fumed that night at Dubrovnik's, calling her every derogatory name he could think of. He was on his third beer and couldn't stop spewing hate. We were gathered around him, taking it all in. The C word and the B word, the stupid this and that. A liberal dose of F. He might have even kept his job if he hadn't barged into his boss's office after he was written up to call him most of the very same names for giving in to that one solitary complainer.

He should've known not to do that from all of our wasted days watching the Cleveland Indians stink up the seventies. No matter how bad the call, never argue with the ump. And especially don't call the ump a stupid F'ng C and tell him he's acting like a B.

The latest Men Without Hats song played loudly on the jukebox while Larry drank and told everyone who would listen what had happened to him. "Hey Larry, if it makes you feel any better, it's a great fucking joke!" someone guffawed, slapping Larry hard on the back. Even Larry laughed then, but it didn't last. He was shaken to his core. We couldn't believe it either. It could've been any of us.

Didn't I just tell Christina the bartender, "Hey, nice ass" when she was bent over restocking the bar? She laughed, though, because she knew I was joking (even though she did have a great ass). She was a tremendous flirt and had already pinched mine when we were punching in the day before. More than pinched. Fondled, I would say. Yes, your honor, it was definitely a fondle.

But what if she hadn't known I was joking? Jesus, that would be tricky. And what about that joke I told about the lion fucking the zebra? We all laughed pretty hard at that. What if someone didn't like seeing free adults enjoying themselves by laughing at a sexual joke? I'd be sent to a reeducation camp . . . er, I mean, a sensitivity seminar. I'd be implicated! *J'accuse!* Collaborator! Jew! Get on the train, sex joker!

Oh my God . . . what if some extremist women's organization was training a whole *army* of uptight, humor-impaired biddies in a secret camp in Idaho to infect every fun-loving workplace in America?

I mean, all it takes to get some quick corporate cash is to convince a jury of people too stupid to get out of jury duty that you were subjected to what a reasonable person would find objectionable, whatever that means. You don't have to get chased around a desk or have your job threatened. You just have to be made uncomfortable by the existence of human sexuality.

Larry started hitting the sauce pretty heavy after that. He tried to fight it, but as soon as he'd get his willpower worked up to walk the straight and narrow, some guy would run into him on the street and shout, "Hey Larry, heard any good ones lately?" Then it was back to his lonely table at Dubrovnik's. He always sat alone during those days.

He had to, the way he was starting to babble to himself half the time.

He was sitting alone at a table in the corner babbling to himself the day I adopted him. No one talked to him much anymore, and he was getting more and more antisocial because of it. The truth is, we were all just tired of him confronting us and asking, "You think you're better'n me?" all the time.

I had just come in with Natalie and was complaining to

Tommy about a particularly cheap table I had the night before. Cheapskates were a common topic of conversation amongst those of us who depended on the kindness of strangers for tips.

". . . and then they left me five bucks! On an eighty-dollar check! After all that running around I had to do. Ketchup for the filet, can you believe those hillbillies? . . . I felt like following them out to the lobby and throwing it at them. Who needs five bucks that bad?" I snorted, waving my hand dismissively and grabbing for my draft beer. In fact, I did need five bucks that bad. Rent was coming up, as well as the car. If I had known that I was now making the best money I'd ever make at Bully's I would've run out into traffic.

"You gotta watch them Canadians," Tommy nodded in agreement. "They don't tip for shit." He grabbed an empty glass from the bar and started to wipe it down. I caught him stealing a look at Natalie's tits.

It happened all the time with her. She was one of those girls with huge tits and a cute face and not much else, so she was always dressing to show them off. She was more woman than I ever dreamed would be attracted to me, and I loved her more than anything. I loved every bit of her, from her Flintstone toes to her chunky thighs right up to her dimpled butt and beyond. Her blue eyes were huge and trusting, and her lips were the fullest and softest I'd ever kissed.

When I made her laugh, she would wrap one arm around her side and hold herself tight while the other arm flailed about wildly. She would squeal, "Ohmigod! Ohmigod, stop! Stop!" and pound the table while I kept making the face or the sound, or whatever the magic thing was that sent her into her convulsions. Those moments were better than sex.

She was also smarter than me, which I found to be a huge turn-on. She kept a 3.5 average at Cleveland State, and would've graduated already if she wasn't forced to only go part-time to take care of her mother.

"Oh, look at poor Larry," she pouted. Out of the corner of my eye I could see that Larry was crying.

"Christ, not again," Tommy muttered.

"Drew, do something." She tugged at my sleeve.

"Uh . . . yeah. Let's get out of here before he sees us and wants to start a conversation."

"Dre-e-ew," she whined, "I mean it! Look at him."

I turned on my barstool and looked to the corner. He was slumped over a table of empty highball glasses, sobbing softly, a string of drool running from his mouth to the table top.

Natalie hurried over to his side. I stayed where I was. You know the old saying: I'd rather have a bottle in front of me than deal with some dumb shit.

I thought if I stared it would just encourage her, so I went back to my beer, wanting to just finish it quickly and go home. Natalie had big plans for me that night, and had been hinting at things to come for the last two days. She wouldn't tell me exactly what it was she wanted to do, but I knew that it involved at least bondage and food. And as long as she didn't just tie me up and shove a carrot up my ass, I was game for anything she could dream up. Especially if she used ice cream the same way she did last time.

When she finally came back she hugged me from behind, snaking her hands down to my crotch, and kissing at my ear. I thought, "Chocolate chip. I hope to God she uses chocolate chip," and then she gave me a suggestive honk through my jeans, letting her hand rub up and down the length of me.

"He's got no place to stay. His parents just kicked him out." Her hands moved up around my chest and held me there.

"And?" My jeans were suddenly looser.

"And my apartment is too small. You have a house."

"*Aaaand?*"

"Aaaaand, you've known him since high school. He's got no place to go, you can't let him sleep on the street." She hugged me tighter, keeping me from jumping up and running out.

"No. No no no. Absolutely not."

Silence. She nestled her face into my shoulder.

"What about the chocolate-chip ice cream and tying me up and everything?" I purred seductively. My last hope was that she was as horny as I was, and would forget all about him to run back to my place and get busy.

"If you let him stay with you, I'll keep my heels on and do it nice and angry."

Larry was grateful for the place to crash, and told me so. About a hundred times.

"Hey, look," I finally had to tell him, "I know you've had some bad times and all, and I don't mind helping you out. But just shut the fuck up about it, will ya?"

"No, man, I mean it." Larry grabbed me by the shoulders and focused his empty eyes directly into mine. He looked like a drug-crazed, maniacal Rasputin. Which was exactly what Rasputin was. A drug-crazed maniac. "I really, really appreciate this man. Really."

"Let me go, man!" I shook loose of him and stepped back. He reeked. I'd been trying to get him to get into the shower but all he wanted to do was tell me how swell I was. "You've been thanking me for an hour. I have to go to sleep."

"No, man, really. Thanks." Larry held out his hand. I thought better of it for a second, and then shook it, not wanting to appear rude.

"You're *welcome*, Larry, don't think anyth—"

He grabbed me in a big smelly bear hug and started crying into my neck, his slobber burning into my skin. "You're the greatest, man! The greatest!" I pictured hundreds of tiny bugs jumping over from him to me, eager for some fresh meat and clean air. "You're a nice man. Nice, nice man."

I decided to burn my clothes. But what about the couch and the extra blankets and pillows I was letting him use? Maybe I could burn them in my backyard. If the cops show up, I'll tell them who'd slept on them and they'll turn the other way.

"Okay man, all right, all right." I tore myself away. Cooties. I'll bet he has cooties. "Sure, sure. Just don't forget to take a shower before you go to sleep, okay? I'll let you know when I'm through."

What the hell, I thought, smelling his residue on me as I walked up the stairs. Maybe I'll take two.

I only put up with the first three days of Larry because of an entire childhood of Presbyterian Sunday school, followed by a Pentecostal junior high and a guilt-ridden high school. He didn't know how lucky he was that I was made to memorize all those Bible verses and watch all those stupid tapes of *Davy and Goliath*. Even though I wasn't much of a practicing Christian at the time, I still believed in eternal damnation and it was only the threat of hell's fire that kept me from throwing Larry back out into the street.

He farted openly. He belched without apology. Every time he blew his nose, which was often, he would follow it up with despicable throat-clearing noises that made me gag. He used all the hot water. He turned up the TV late at night when I had to get up early the next day. He yelled at the screen during movies he'd already seen. "Don't go in the basement! Look out behind you! He's got a gun!" He borrowed money to buy booze that I couldn't afford to loan and knew I wouldn't get back.

For the next four days, I put up with Larry only because Natalie threatened to quit letting me go down on her if I let anything happen to that poor, poor man. I knew she was serious because she had shut down the buffet for a whole week once after she'd found some skin magazines under my mattress. She was "morally opposed" to any of her men masturbating. She felt that it was insulting to her sexuality, and had made me throw away my whole collection when we started to get serious.

Larry continued his previous bad behavior, but in a more comfortable way. He was getting used to living there, no longer even asking, "Hey, mind if I check the fridge?" before diving in like a bear into a picnic basket.

He had skipped a couple of bath times now that he was more relaxed, and his drinking increased. And why wouldn't it? It's not like he had a job to go to or anything.

On Larry's sixth day with me, Miss Liberace seated me three tables in a row inside of five minutes, just to be a bitch. I was working section two that night, so everyone he gave me was a VIP. The third table he gave me was headed by the wife of the guy who owned a local sports franchise (now defunct), and she wasn't looking too happy about having been made to wait her turn.

"I'll have a manhattan, fruit on a side plate, off the skewer please. And a side of ice in a water glass." Her rich lady friends had ordered in a similar vein, probably expecting me to carry each of their orders out on a separate silver tray. She barely looked at me when she ordered her drink, adding, "And let's see . . . " while she looked at the appetizer menu.

I stood there, itchy-footed, waiting for her to peruse the selections. I had two more tables to fetch drinks for, food to deliver, and oh shit, here comes Liberace with another deuce!

"Oh . . . I don't know . . ." she chirped, the loose skin of her neck flapping wildly like a skull and crossbones on a pirate ship.

Don't know what? I thought to myself. Don't know why you don't just go ahead and get another face-lift? Or are you afraid your ears would disappear? Don't know why you look like you buy your makeup from an undertaker? Hurry the fuck up! The new table has already motioned me to come over when I'm through with you and I haven't even been to the bar to get the drink orders I took before I got stuck with you. I already know you don't tip, so hurry the fuck up!!!

"Oh . . . I'll just wait until after my drink gets here." Another pause while she folded her bony hands into her lap. "Remember, fruit on a side plate, off the skewer. Side of ice in a water glass. Can you remember that?"

I cocked my head and gave her my most confident, can-do smile. "C-c-coming r-r-ight up, m-m-m-ma'am."

My first stutter.

I got to Dubrovnik's Tavern that night about midnight. My nerves were shot and I couldn't stand the thought of going home to Larry and no Natalie. She hadn't been returning my calls for the last couple of days, but I left a message on her machine to meet me here if she got it in time.

Right away, I noticed a big white board over by the pool tables. Looking closer, I saw that it was a giant calendar of April, and there were names all over it with 5s and 10s written next to the names in red marker. "What's that?" I asked Tommy, ordering up a Bud.

"Oh, man, it's like I had a stroke of genius!" he enthused, shaking my hand. "You're going to make someone a lot of money. Here, this one's on me."

Then Tommy explained his whole great idea. Larry had been

with me long enough to start some speculating amongst the boys at the bar. How long will it last? How's Drew going to get rid of him? Stuff like that.

So Tommy decided to start a pool. No one thought it could last through the next month, so he made this giant calendar, and let people buy dates that they thought Larry would get thrown out on. There was a five-dollar pool, a ten-dollar pool, a twenty-dollar pool, a fifty-dollar pool, and a hundred-dollar pool. It was similar to the kind of football pools that went on during football season. If you picked the right date, you got all the money in that pool, minus the five percent the bar kept for running it. I noticed that the earliest dates were all gone already.

"And what do I get?" I asked him.

"Oh no. You're not allowed to bet. Larry either. If you did, you could just throw him out on whatever date you picked." Tommy liked to think he was the world's greatest worker of angles.

"Yeah, no shit. I mean, I'm the guy having to put up with Larry all this time and I don't get a percentage or anything?"

"What? Hey, we bet on the Browns all the time and don't give them a cut. What's your problem?" Now he was worried that I was going to complain and hurt his business.

Out of nowhere, I said, "If I could go the whole month without kicking him out then *I* should get all the money." I wasn't thinking about it, I just said it.

"And if you don't?" Tommy stopped wiping and cocked his head.

I quickly did the math. Thirty times five, thirty times ten, thirty times twenty, thirty times fifty, thirty times a hundred . . . holy shit! Natalie and I could get married on that kind of money. Not that we ever seriously discussed it, but . . . I was giddy. A down payment on a new car. Some new clothes. A new attitude with Miss Liberace the next time he sat me three tables in a row and got Mrs. Moneybags pissed at me because her fruit or her manhattan wasn't right.

I could do this standing on my head for that kind of money. "Well, I'll tell you what!" Why didn't I just shut up? Why? "If I lose, I'll double all the bets that are up there at the time. I'll give you the pink slip to my car as collateral." There. That oughta fill up the board pretty quick, and by the end of the month I'd have five thousand five hundred and fifty tax-free dollars in my pocket.

A cheer went up. Tommy pointed a finger at me, laughing. "You're *on*, stupid!"

I pointed a finger back at him and smiled wickedly, yelling to everyone at the bar.

"No, *you're* on, mother*fucker*! Gimme a drink!"

God, I loved being cocky and right. Five thousand five hundred and fifty bucks. I had the world by the balls.

"Motherfucker! Motherfucker! Oh . . . mother*fucker*!" It was Natalie's voice, but it couldn't be. She never used that kind of language. "Damn! Oh damn! Ooooooh!! I can't believe your doing this to me! Damn!"

Uh oh, trouble. It was up to me to save her! I took the stairs to my house two at time and raced to the sound to rescue my baby. The love of my life.

When I ran through the open bedroom door I saw the face of evil. The most heinous, foul, depraved act against nature that I had ever witnessed: Natalie, astride Larry's face facing his feet, tweaking his nipples and humping herself into him like she was in the Kentucky Derby. My favorite position.

The sounds that were coming out of her were like none I had ever heard come out of any human being. Ever. Not to say that she was the silent type, far from it. But she never sounded more animalistic and gutteral, ranting in satanic mewlings accented with the bestial howls of a celebrated kill. Her face was contorted into a tight mask of agony as her mind sought to regain control of her body.

And Larry. I didn't even like seeing him with his shirt off, much less with everything else uncovered. And of all the grotesque things about the way he looked; the odd tufts of hair, the strange lesions, the red splotchy patches of dried skin . . . nothing was worse than what stuck out from between his legs. It was like a miniature fat, bald man wearing bear-claw slippers. I wanted to gouge my eyes out at the sight of it. Its only saving grace, if you could call it that, was that it was uncommonly huge. Which is like saying that Mt. Everest is kind of big for a mountain. I'd been in the Boy Scouts, The Marine Corps, and a college fraternity, and I've never seen anything that big in any shower room, not that I ever looked.

And then she saw me. She sat up abruptly, covering her bosom with her hands.

"Oh," was all she said to me before I stormed out.

I went to Kenny King's and had a cup of coffee to settle my nerves before heading back. Larry was on the couch, picking at his toes like nothing had happened.

"Hey! How's it goin', chief?" he smiled at me. I walked past him and up to my room without saying a word. She hadn't told him. He didn't see me walk in because her ass was over his eyes, and she didn't tell him. Or maybe she did and he was just being a bigger prick than I thought he was.

I stuttered pretty much the whole next day. Larry asked if there was anything he could do to help me with it. "I know a lot about herbal medicine and stuff, man. Just let me know," he said, taking a big swig of gin.

Oh, thanks pal. And why don't you go fuck yourself? Your dick's big enough.

Of course I didn't say that. The betting board at Dubrovnik's had totally filled up in just twenty-four hours, even the hundred dollar spots, and I couldn't afford to pay off the bets if I lost.

I had to go opening my stupid mouth, didn't I? "I'll cover *all* your bets, mother*fucker!*" What a dope.

Hey, here's a tip for you: The next time you have the world by the balls, don't twist them.

In the meantime, it was more of the same at my house. Goddamn Larry. Larry ruined my home. Larry ruined my job. Larry took my Natalie.

Natalie.

Natalie kept coming over like nothing had happened. I would leave to go to work. She would stay.

I saw no reason to be civil to Larry after that, except for the fact that he now held my short-term financial future in his dirty little tit-squeezing hands. So, I was only as civil as I needed to be.

"Hey Drew," he would ask, "can you loan me twenty bucks tonight?"

"Sure thing, asswipe," I would reply in my head, cheerily. "Why don't you blow me and I'll get right on that for you?" When in fact, I would just reach into my wallet silently and give it to him, hoping I could outlast the horror long enough to collect the bar pool and get my bills caught up again.

After a week, I noticed the extra hair in my comb. It coincided with Larry's new fondness for walking in on me while I was seated on the commode. I would've locked the door, but he had broken the lock in a drunken rampage, yelling something about pirates.

During the second week, I began to bite my nails again, a

habit I thought I had beaten in college. I was biting them right down to a bloody stump. That started after Larry announced on the front porch at three in the morning that he was an alcoholic. Like we were all wondering.

He had gotten hold of a pamphlet that was in my bag from a comic book convention. I had gone there just to get out of the house and away from him for awhile. The pamphlet was from the Cleveland Cares Foundation and was entitled "Are You an Alcoholic?" In it were ten trick questions like, "Would you rather drink than make love to your wife?" and Larry had answered yes to all ten of them.

This caused him to run right out to the front porch dressed in nothing but his boxers with a near empty bottle of Jack Daniel's in his hands. "Yes!" he screamed, pumping his fists in to the air. "Yes! Yes! *Yes!*" Lights started coming on across the street as I ran downstairs to see what the hell was going on.

"YES! I'M AN ALCOHOLIC! WHOOOOOOOO! I'M AN ALCOHOLIC AND YOU CAN ALL KISS MY FAT ALCOHOLIC ASS! WHOOOOO!"

During week three, I was questioned openly at Dubrovnik's about Larry's relationship with Natalie. "She says he's hung like a five-legged Clydesdale," offered one of my drinking pals.

"And his tongue ain't bad either, she says," offered another.

I offered them my ass and vowed not to come back unless it was to get all of their stinking money.

During week four, I was fired. Not that I blamed them. I stuttered full-time by then, my fingernails were grotesque to look at, and my hands shook when I set the drinks down on the tables. It was even too much for the customers in the lows, and some of them had been complaining.

By then, Larry was looking like an evil, last-days Howard Hughes. His drinking had gotten so bad that he just grunted and squealed when you were trying to talk to him, and grunted and squealed even more when you weren't. Even Natalie didn't come around to see him anymore. I think.

The last straw at work was when Denise, one of the owners, came across me standing by the back window and staring out across the river to the Flats. The shift had just started and no-body cheap-looking enough to be seated in the lows had come in yet.

"Don't you have side work to do?" she snipped at me, like a Spaniard to an Indian. "I don't pay you to just stand around, you know."

I kept staring. She and her husband paid me two dollars an hour. The rest I made in tips. "Hey bitch, you know what?" I said softly, never taking my eyes off the bright lights of the cars snaking in and out of the Flats. Cars that were on their way to fun and sex and everything else I no longer had. "Fuuuuuuck you." The words came out tonelessly, and with a blush of anger. Finally, my stutter was gone. And so was I.

I had only four more days to go before the bet was over. The money would soon be mine, but so what? It wasn't enough to last forever. Would I get my mind back before my money was gone? Would I ever get another waiter job after what I said to the owner of the most expensive restaurant in town? And by the way, how do stuttering, no-job guys get laid in Cleveland anyway?

Kill yourself, I thought. You'll never amount to anything now, so just kill yourself. You'll have to go back to being a fucking *busboy*, you loser! You're almost thirty! You'll be taking the 20B *bus* downtown to get to your stinking *busboy* job. Ha ha ha! Yeah, you'll meet lots of women on the bus! Fat hillbilly chicks in giant shift dresses because they can't fit into pants any-more. And they'll only fuck you because they feel sorry for you.

Just like Natalie felt sorry for Larry! Haaaa! Hee hee hee! Stop it! My sides! Oh, my God . . . that's funny. Hey! Maybe she's riding his face right now, making those same noises. Making that same face. The things you could never get her to do on your best day. And she never had any trouble wrapping two hands around anything that stuck out from your body, now did she? No woman ever will. Go kill yourself.

Or better yet . . . kill Larry.

A calmness quickly came over me. A shudder of tranquility that I hadn't felt since giving myself over to the Lord at the altar of the Bethany Assembly of God on Memphis Avenue.

Yeah, man. Kill Larry.

I ran out the door as quickly as I could to Video 21 on Pearl Road and rented as many murder mysteries as I could find, looking for tips. I watched them on a portable video player in a cheap motel room.

The next day, it was the hardware store at Pearl and State and a rental place in Parma for supplies. I kept them in my trunk until the last moment. I had to be careful that Larry didn't stumble across my plan accidentally, because he was now wandering randomly around the house and going through my stuff when he drank, and he drank all the time. We can't take the chance that he would stumble upon our little party unexpectedly, can we? And what if some of his deductive reasoning brain cells are still alive?

The last day. 7:00 P.M. After moving Larry's high school boxes out of the way, I unpacked everything and laid it out neatly under the basement window. (Oh, it was so grand to be neat again! Sweet freedom! And it was just hours away!) Taking off my shirt, I started in on the floor. The pickax was loud, but it didn't take many swings to get the cheap cement to come loose. Then, working feverishly, I dug a hole about three feet long and three feet deep. I didn't make it any longer because I wanted the satisfaction of carving up his body after I killed him, and why waste your energy digging a bigger grave than you really need?

9:00 P.M. The industrial acid and fresh cement mix were the next items to come out of their bags. I didn't have to mix the cement yet, but I wanted the hose and trough ready to go anyway.

The acid was in a big gallon jug like milk comes in. The guy at the store never asked me what it was for or anything. I don't know what I would've told him if he did. "I'm going to pour it over my pal Larry's stupid ugly face after I kill him to get all of my old lady's beaver sap off of it, whaddya think I'm going to do with a gallon of acid? Ha ha ha!" Like normal people buy acid all the time. But, you needed to be "at least eighteen years of age and able to prove it" to buy a can of spray paint. What a country.

10:30 P.M. Larry staggers in, drunk as usual.

"Heeey, roomie! Haaaaaa ha ha . . . ," he gurgled. "Big day today! Big day today!" He made to hug me and I let him.

"Yeah, man!" I smiled. "Hey! Let's go to Dubrovnik's and celebrate! I'm buyin!" I said it like I hadn't been already buying him all his booze for the last five weeks.

12:01 A.M. Cheers break out at Dubrovnik's while Tommy counts out my money. They all count along. "One thousand! Two thousand! Three thousand! Four thousand! Five thousand!" I tip Larry a hundred and slap him on the back. Pandemonium. Laughter. I buy all the drinks. No one feels better than I do.

I waited until dawn to do it. We had closed Dubrovnik's, and I had a couple of bottles waiting for us when we got home so as not to stop the celebration too soon. One bottle filled with vodka for him, and one bottle filled with store-bought drinking water for me.

I pretended to be just as drunk as he was, dancing around to the radio, giggling at everything he said, and generally falling all over myself like I'd seen him do so many times. For that one night, I was his bestest and funniest pal. True blue, buddy! Gotcherback!

As the darkness of the night was turning gray, he excused himself to go upstairs and abuse the bathroom. When he didn't come down for ten minutes, I figured he had finally passed out, and reached under the sofa cushions for the weapon.

Thanks to our nation's restrictive gun laws, my weapon of choice was the biggest fucking hunting knife I could find. It was either that or wait two weeks while they did a background check on me at the gun store and I didn't want to have Larry around any longer than I had to.

It was heavy and cold, with a shiny, leather-covered handle. A ten-inch, self-contained death delivery system made of the finest Detroit steel. Death in my hands.

When I got upstairs to my room, I found Larry naked, rocking back and forth on his knees, facing the first light of day through the dusty window. The curtains were balled in the corner where he had used them to clean up some bloody vomit. "I'm going to stab you extra for that, you fucking hillbilly," I whispered to myself.

I was naked, too, to make it easier to clean up his blood, and as I tiptoed closer I could hear him talking to himself. He had the "Are You an Alcoholic?" pamphlet in his hand, giggling. He was taking the quiz again!

Self-realization won't save you now, you smelly, never-flushing, girlfriend-stealing piece of dog shit. I'm already naked. I already spent money on a knife. I have death in my hands. Death in my hands. Death in my hands . . .

Larry took a giant swig of vodka, leaned backward, and saw me. He had sores on his forehead and dried blood caked around his nose. "Hey, man," he slurred, his eyebrows bunching up into a question mark.

Death . . . in . . . my . . . hands. . . .

I lunged at him.

And pushed him out the window.

Larry bounced once, and ended up with a concussion, a broken arm, cracked ribs, and various scratches and contusions. Don't ask me why I never stabbed him, because I don't know. Maybe you should ask the Bethany Assembly of God on Memphis Avenue.

I never spent a night in jail.

While we were on the way to Deaconess Hospital in my car, I told Larry that he fell, and in his drunken pain he believed me, although he never looked at me the same after that.

I took a week to sleep and clean, unplugging my phone and only leaving my house to go to Lawson's for pop and snack food. Then I spent another week just watching TV. I finally got a job at the Denny's out in Independance waiting tables on the graveyard shift.

Natalie never called me again.

THE

ROYAL

Rent money. That's what my life was all about that year. Making the stupid rent money. Every night, working the graveyard shift at the stupid Denny's on the stupid Strip waiting on stupid Las Vegas tourists that were too stupid to go to a buffet where the food was better and cheaper.

Every night, eight hours of waiting on those people. Eight hours of looking at dirty orange leatherette and stained Formica. Eight hours surrounded by incompetent managers who sat around and smoked cigarettes while I was swamped with angry customers yelling, "Where's my coffee?" and, "What're they doin' back there, killing the cow?"

All so I could pay some rent.

If I had money, I could just pay my rent as an afterthought, and live for the girlfriend I didn't currently have or the hobbies I couldn't afford at the moment. But I didn't.

All I could do was pay my two hundred and eighty-five dollars a month for a furnished studio apartment downtown, which included a bad color TV. No cable. Couldn't even get it if you wanted it because there was no hookup available. The furniture was ratty, the toilet ran, and the drug-dealing neighbors were loud. Meeting the rent was the sole reason for my existence on earth.

I thought about this as I walked up Fremont Street to the main bus stop downtown where I would catch the # 6 bus to the Strip and start my eight hours among the damned. It was nine o'clock at night and ninety degrees out. I was glad to see that it had cooled off from the day, when it had gotten up to one hundred and twelve.

I had just started walking and it would be another twenty-five minutes before I got to the bus stop. Five days a week I made this walk, sometimes six. And then I made the walk back. The whole time I walked, I thought about how rotten I had it and about how I regretted ever having moved here.

I discovered Las Vegas the year before on a Greyhound bus trip that I had taken from Cleveland to see my brother Neal in California. I would sleep on the bus at night and wash up in the sink in the bus station men's rooms in the morning. All I had for luggage was a backpack.

I was nineteen.

The bus rides were spent mostly in silence, because Walkmans hadn't been invented yet. All I did was stare out of the window at total desert darkness until I got sleepy, thinking about how if I had just bothered to show up for class once in a while, I wouldn't have been kicked out of school. I wouldn't have even had to study that hard. They were only freshman courses, after all. All I would've had to do was show up and pay attention and get by, and I didn't even do that.

My first image of Las Vegas was at night, which is the best way for it to happen. The bus station was downtown next to the Union Plaza, which was at the very top of Fremont Street. Fremont Street is the one you see on TV that's always lit up so much it looks like daytime at three in the morning.

I never saw so many lights, or so much money, and I needed more of both. I was living there by the end of the year.

Gambling, I decided in that one day in Vegas, was going to be the way I would make my mark in the world. I imagined myself turning pro and living an underground life on the edge of society, with no social security number or known address. A Las Vegas hipster with inside knowledge. A player. The man who knows what he knows and isn't telling you.

Oh, I had big dreams back then.

I would live in a one-bedroom condo just off the Strip, complete with cable and a leather couch that I would pick out myself. I'd even put some money down and get one of those great new Sony Beta machines that had just come out. I'd be able to buy new clothes from the mall instead of having to wear only the clothes I got for Christmas and my birthday all the time. And when I went to the casinos, I'd drive my brand-new used Datsun Z into the valet, tipping the kid a five-dollar bill without even blinking. If I wanted a sandwich at the coffee shop, I'd just buy it. I'd buy beer by the bottle instead of draft. And the women . . . I was going to be big, big, big.

Okay, so they weren't big dreams. But they were to me.

Besides, I was only twenty. It was illegal for me to be gambling anyway.

But there I was, almost every day. At the blackjack table trying to count cards, at the craps table betting some new progressive system I'd dreamt up, or at the sports book trying to beat a point spread.

I thought that the reason I wasn't going anywhere was because of the small stakes I was forced to play due to the unfortunate state of my initial cash flow situation. All I needed to become a full-time player was to move up in class, that's all. Just a little mo' money, and I would be good to go.

You gotta bet big to win big, that was the saying in Vegas. The moon is made of cheese. The social security system is sound. We can win the war in Vietnam. Koo koo ga joob.

That morning after I got home from work, I counted my cash. One hundred and twenty dollars from the last four days. I had one hundred and five in the bank.

Two hundred and twenty-five dollars.

Not as much as I was counting on to pay my two hundred and eighty-five-dollar rent.

Yesterday was Friday the third, the very last and final day I could pay my rent without being late. I had just written a check to the apartment manager for the two eighty-five, which was going to be deposited on Monday. So now, I had Saturday night and all day Sunday to wonder how in the hell I was going to get out of this one. Luckily, I had those days off so I couldn't make any more money in tips while trying to figure out how to get ahold of sixty dollars in Vegas, plus a little extra so I could eat.

The stupid rent.

It wouldn't have been such a problem, but the apartment manager was a no-nonsense, by-the-rules type who had already

warned me that if I was late with the rent one more time she
would have to throw me out. She didn't want to, but those
were the rules. She had told me so in a crisp, formal tone of
voice, like the one you hear when you call the phone company
to get the correct time. The same tone of voice she used to say
"Good morning," or "Have a nice day."

At the tone, the time will be rent time. And not one second
later.

The only recollection I have of her saying anything remotely
familiar to me was when I passed her office one day to get a
Pepsi while I was laying by the pool, and she said, "Hey, you
look good out there in your little swimsuit."

"Uh, thanks," I think I told her.

Now, if I was a twenty-year-old woman and the apartment
manager was a man, I knew what I'd do without even thinking
about it. But that's because women can fake sexual enjoyment.
My apartment manager was a bony, ugly, sixty-three-year-old
woman, so there was no way. Besides, all I needed was sixty
dollars. What's that for a near professional gambler like me?

Needing sixty more dollars for rent was a godsend, really. At
the moment, my favorite game of chance was poker. Seven card
stud. I'd been playing at the one-to-four dollar tables and only
losing about twenty dollars a session, so I thought I was pretty
good.

I'd wanted to move up to the big boys at the five-ten tables
for a while, and now I had my excuse. You've got to bet big to
win big. I would just win the money. Koo Koo Ga Joob.

I decided to play at the Horseshoe, my favorite downtown
casino. Binion's Horseshoe Hotel and Casino was one of the
first "name" casinos in the downtown area. It was built by
Benny Binion, a gambler from Dallas who ran illegal dice games
there. He'd wanted to build on the Strip, but the mob wouldn't

let him. Rumor has it he'd killed a man in Texas, and that's why he had to come to Nevada to try his luck in the first place. His smiling face is on every chip in the casino. The smile of a man who has gotten away with something, but you're not sure what.

The Horseshoe is also the home of the World Series of Poker, held there every year in May, so if you really want to do some serious poker playing, the Horseshoe is the place to go.

The sounds of a poker room in Las Vegas are like no other in a casino. The incessant smacking of chips being shuffled together, the steady backbeat of names being called out when seats become free . . . "DJ for twenty-forty Hold 'Em! Last call for DJ, twenty-forty Hold 'Em!"

At the tables themselves, there's not much conversation going on outside the game, except at the ones with the lower limits. There, people talk too much. They love to discuss how you should've played your last hand when you're sitting at the one-four tables. They love asking me things like, "Why'd you stay in when you knew I had kings?" Or else they'll discuss me in the third person with somebody else at the table.

"Well, when I saw that guy catch the heart on fifth street, I knew he had to have it. I already had queens up and was trying to fill, but this guy," pointing to me, "I don't know what he was thinking. I thought maybe he had rolled up trips or something." Then they would ask me, "Did you have trips?" Like a professional would divulge his tactics to the other people at his table.

"You can read all about what I think when I write my book, you nosy asshole," I would think to myself. I knew I'd be good enough at poker to write one someday. *Drew's Power Plus Poker System* I would call it. All the top players wrote a book.

I sauntered up to the poker room manager and had him put

my name on the five-ten stud list. I'd never asked to be on the five-ten list before, and it thrilled me. I was finally moving up in the ranks.

There were ten names ahead of mine. There was also a waiting list for one-four stud, ten-twenty stud, and all of the Hold 'Em and Omaha Hi-Lo games, so there were quite a few of us loitering around the manager's podium waiting for our names to be called. We all smoked, swapped poker stories, and traded hot tips on horses. No one seemed to mind in the least about waiting, or seemed in any kind of big hurry. We were all brothers in cards. Of course, these same fraternal poker mates of mine would have an ace-high shit fit if they waited an extra minute for coffee at Denny's. Especially if I was serving them.

After about a twenty minute wait, I was led to a table and seated just across from the dealer. This was a great seat for me to have, because I could see all the cards on the oblong table without straining myself. I gave a cursory nod to my table mates and whipped out my flash roll. One hundred and twenty dollars in fives and singles. Four days worth of tips. The dealer looked like she was going to kill me, and the other five players didn't look all that happy about it either.

It took her a minute or so to lay it all out for the overhead cameras. She never once looked up at me or acknowledged my existence. She must have felt my pro vibe and was trying to be respectful.

"Change one-twenty!" she announced, and pushed a stack of red chips my way. A small stack, which kind of threw me. In my head, I always thought that a hundred and twenty in five-dollar chips would look bigger.

I threw my first five-dollar chip out for the ante. It hopped across the felt and landed on the floor behind the dealer. I stared at my hands in the coolest way I could manage while someone retrieved it and the dealer made change, pushing four one-dollar chips and a two quarters back at me.

Now, you always want to keep track of the pot while you play each hand so you can figure your profit if you win. (That would be the first lesson in my book.) There were three dollars and fifty cents in the pot so far, fifty cents of it mine. So, I automatically subtracted the three dollar percentage that the house will probably take out of the pot by the end of the hand, for a profit of . . . nothing. Only sixty dollars to go.

In seven card stud, you get three cards to start with, two dealt facedown, and the third faceup. If you stay in the hand for all seven cards, you use your best five as your hand. I was dealt a three-card flush, all spades. A ten and a jack down, with a three showing. I had four more cards to try and get two spades. Not too bad. I didn't expect to have a playable hand so early in the game. It wasn't unusual in seven card stud to sit for an hour or more waiting for a good hand that you could jump in with. Maybe today was my lucky day.

"Deuce of clubs," the dealer yawned, motioning her hand to the player to her right, an elderly black man in a ratty old sweater. In casino poker games, the lowest card always has to start things rolling with some kind of small bet. It's called the bring-in bet, and in five-ten stud, it's a dollar.

"Damn," the old guy said, chuckling and throwing in his dollar chip. "Damn my luck all day."

The old white guy sitting to his right in a blue T-shirt and a "Hilton Poker Room" baseball cap had an ace of hearts showing. "Make it five," he said, and the game was on.

The guy between us was next. He was a young, fresh-faced Mormon-looking kid in an Izod shirt with the collar turned up. Some college geek. He had a six of diamonds showing and folded immediately. He had a dollar chip in his hand when he did, so I knew that he would have bet the bring-in amount if the guy with the ace hadn't raised right away. That's a common trick if you have an ace showing on the first three cards. You raise the bet immediately as if you have a pair of aces, even if you have nothing else, trying to get everyone at the table to fold right off the bat so that you can "steal" the ante. And Mr. Six wasn't going to go up against an ace this early, especially not for five dollars, so he was out.

I called, hoping to stay in and catch the rest of my spade flush, ruining Mr. Ace's ploy to steal the ante. A three-flush isn't a favorite against a possible pair of aces, but if you just call the bets and don't try anything fancy, you might get lucky and win in the end. My hand shook as I tossed my chip out. Five dollars on one bet. Jesus. That's a day's worth of food in Las Vegas. I hoped nobody had noticed the shaky hand, but I'm sure Mr. Ace had.

The next two bettors, a younger black guy in a muscle T-shirt with no muscles and a king of hearts, and a middle-aged Asian guy with a jack of clubs, called.

The last player, an olive-skinned woman to the dealer's immediate left, had the queen of hearts and did the same. She looked like she was in her late thirties, still fairly attractive but with a hard face. Probably a burned-out cocktail waitress, I thought. When this was all over, maybe I'd buy her a drink and try to get lucky.

The old black dude with the deuce stayed in too, putting in four more dollars to get his bet to five, but I didn't know why. No wonder his luck was running so bad. He was stupid.

Thirty-three dollars in the pot, and we were only on third street. Jesus, that's a lot of money, I thought. In the games I was used to playing, that was a big pot, and we were only just now getting started.

Fourth street. We get our fourth cards.

Four of clubs for Mr. Deuce of clubs. Oh, I get it, I thought. He's going for a flush, just like me. Well, you better have a queen under there, old man, because I got a big old Jackson throbbing under my hand right now, and the Chinese-looking guy already has your jack of clubs that you need to keep up with me.

An eight of clubs for Mr. Ace. No help to him, but it takes another club out of play for Mr. Deuce, so it helps me.

A queen of spades for me. Now I'm four cards into a flush with three to go. Better have a king of clubs now, you old dummy. Keep putting your money in the pot.

A ten of hearts for Mr. King, the young, black, skinny dude. Another possible flush? Then an eight for Mr. Jack, and a seven for the fading beauty I was starting to get the hots for, the Queen of Hearts.

"Ace," said the dealer. Now the high card starts the betting. He bet five, I called, Mr. King called making me sure he was going for a flush, Mr. Jack and the Queen of Hearts folded, and Mr. "I'm So Damn Unlucky" deuce of clubs called. Who did he think he was fooling with that "damn my luck" shit? Maybe that works with the tourists at the one-four tables, but not here. This is the five-ten table, buddy. The big time.

Fifty-three dollars in the pot, ten-fifty of it mine. Forty-two dollars and fifty cents profit if the game ended right now. The fifth card had yet to be dealt, and already there was almost rent sitting right in front of me. Man, I could make my rent in one hand! I suddenly loved playing for high stakes. C'mon, spades! One more spade! One more spade!

Fifth street. An important round, because the bet doubles automatically. A two of spades to Mr. I'm So Damn Unlucky. Sheee-it! That was the one I needed. Oh well, at least he didn't get his club. Maybe now he'll drop out.

A three of clubs to the guy in the Hilton Poker Room hat, Mr. Ace. Hah! I bet that hurt, Mr. Unlucky. C'mon spades!

A three of hearts to me. Shit, shit, and double shit. Where the hell are all the spades?

Queen of diamonds to Mr. King, who needs hearts. Well, Jesus, we're all getting screwed here, aren't we? Now I don't feel so bad.

"Ace is still high," said the dealer, who was turning out to be quite a conversationalist.

"Ten," says Mr. Ace, tossing in two chips.

"Call," I say, noticing that the pot is near rent-ready.

"Call," says Mr. King.

"Raise it," says Mr. Unlucky Deuce, throwing in twenty in chips.

Raise it? Raise it?! What the hell? What does he got there? A two of clubs, a four of clubs, and a two of spades . . . oh, I get it now. I read about this in one of my books.

He wants us to think he's got three twos when he's really going for the flush! He's raising the bet hoping that me and the other guy that are going for the same hand will see that and fold, afraid of him filling up into a full house. Nice try, old timer. I'll show you how to bluff some cards.

Mr. Ace calls the bet. I reach into my pile of chips.

"Reraise," I say. And, trying not to shake too much, put twenty more dollars in the pot for a total of thirty. Thirty dollars. Eight hours work for me. Eight hours of "Where's my coffee?" and, "There's something sticky on my table." Jesus. High stakes, indeed.

I winked at the washed-out cocktail waitress as I bet my money. She winked back. Everybody loves a winner.

Everyone called my bet. I'd lost track of how much was in the pot, but I knew that it was plenty. Over one-fifty, for sure.

Rent and a prime rib. Maybe a new pair of jeans. All I knew for sure now is what I had left, because every time I looked down, I counted it. Seventy-nine dollars and fifty cents.

Sixth street. I'm golden. Mr. Unlucky Deuce gets a seven of diamonds. No help in either direction.

Mr. Ace gets the ace of hearts. Now he has two aces showing, but it doesn't matter, because my king of spades! gives me a king high flush which easily beats the three aces he probably has. Queen, ten, jack, three, and now . . . the king. Five happy spades. Get ready to push the money to a player.

Mr. King gets a three of hearts, which probably helps him get his king high flush, but it still doesn't matter because I also have a queen and a jack. His next highest card is a ten. I'll win the tiebreaker. Maybe I'll take the olive-skinned babe to a motel. One with dirty movies on closed-circuit TV.

"Pair of aces." The dealer doesn't seem excited by any of this. She's a robot. Cold and soulless. Nice chest, though. Man, winning gets me horny.

Mr. Aces checks. He knows me and Mr. King both have a flush, and has to wait for us to bet so he can fold.

I can barely contain my excitement. "Ten," I say giddily.

Mr. King calls. I figure he doesn't know if he has the extra cards he needs to beat me, but can't throw away a flush. Good. More money for me.

"Raise it," says Mr. Deuce, throwing in another twenty. Then, before I had a chance to say, "What the hell?", Mr. Ace pipes up.

"Reraise," he said, tossing in thirty dollars.

Reraise? Wha—? The sonuvabitch check-raised us! He checked, like he didn't have anything, just so we would all bet and give him a chance to raise us and sweeten the pot. A check-raise! One of the lowest, dirtiest tricks you can pull.

You're gonna check-raise three aces against a flush? I thought, glaring at him. Not against me, you're not! Those two at that end of the table were really pissing me off. Raising with deuces, check-raising with aces . . . I'll put a stop to this bullshit right now!

"Raise it again." I grabbed forty more dollars and threw it in the pot. This was make or break time. Miss Queen of Hearts gave me a look that shot right through my eyeballs, went screaming down my spine, and landed in my pants. I had twenty-nine dollars left. And fifty cents.

"Call," said Mr. King after thinking it over. He was still afraid of throwing the flush away. It took him a second or two just to count up the forty dollars that he needed to get even with the rest of us. He was shaking his head in disbelief the whole time he did it.

"Reraise," said Mr. Deuce, and threw in forty more of his own. A line in the sand.

"Reraise again," said Mr. Ace, more annoyed than anything else. I think he did it just for spite.

The bet was now seventy, just for this round. I had already put in fifty, plus what was already in there. I couldn't think. All I knew was that I was in too deep now to stop. I put in my last twenty-nine dollars. "I'm all in," I whispered.

All in. All except for two quarters that I had only because the dealer waved them off. I stuffed them into my pocket.

One hundred and nineteen dollars and fifty cents of my rent money. Over five hundred dollars total in the pot. All riding on a king-high flush.

Everyone else at the table just called. It happens sometimes, in poker, that everyone decides that enough money is on the table, and they just want the hand to end so they can see who the better man is. This was one of those times.

The last card was dealt facedown. We all took our cards without looking at them. Mr. Ace checked, I checked, and so did Mr. King and Mr. Deuce. We just wanted to see who had what and get it over with.

"Let's see 'em," said the dealer, setting the deck down on the felt.

Mr. Ace was first. "Aces full of eights," he said calmly, dragging on a cigarette. A full house. I was numb. A full house beats a flush like Clay beat Liston. I never saw it coming, either. I was right about his three aces, but totally misread the rest of it. My rent money was gone. The only reason I had to be alive. Gone.

I was already dreading the call to my mother.

Mr. King didn't have to show his hand at all, since he was as beat as I was, but he did anyway. He had a king-high heart flush, just like I thought it would be. His next highest card after the king was a jack, just like I thought it would be. He looked embarrassed flipping the cards over. "It's the best hand I had all night. Couldn't bear to throw it away," he said sheepishly. Mr. Ace chuckled good-naturedly at him. Well, at least I read one hand right, I thought.

The old black dude, Mr. Deuce, smiled broadly at all of us. "Four deuces," he sang, flipping his down cards over with a flourish. "I had rolled-up trips from the git-go!" He rubbed his hands together eagerly.

Mr. Ace stopped chuckling and looked up at the ceiling. I heard him say "shit" under his breath. Mr. I'm So Damn Unlucky had played his hand perfectly, and we all missed it.

"Man, I never saw that coming," I said, trying to smile while I turned my own cards over. I didn't have to show my hand either, but I wanted Mr. King to see them. I had him beat, at least, and wanted him to know it before I started my long walk home to the apartment I was going to get kicked out of on Monday if my mom couldn't wire me any money.

"I have king-high spades with a queen, a ten, a jack, and an . . . ace."

My last down card was an ace. An ace of spades. I had a spade royal flush!

"Oh my God! I've got a royal!" My hands flew up into my face in disbelief. "A royal flush! Oh my God!" A couple of the players at the other tables heard my yelling and stood up to look. A small round of applause broke out as the news made its way around the poker room.

Mr. Deuce looked straight ahead at nothing in particular. "Goddamn," he said. "A goddamn royal flush."

The dealer smiled and pushed the chips toward me. There were too many to count. All I know is that they were all red, and they were all beautiful. I tossed five of them at the dealer.

"More where that came from," I laughed.

"What did you say your name was, honey?" the Queen of Hearts asked me from across the table. Her voice was nice and raspy. A smoky, sexy kind of low that turned me on to no end.

"It's Drew. Drew Carey. What's yours?" I couldn't wait to kiss her.

"Shawnetta." She smiled at me and lit a cigarette.

Hmmm. An Italian chick named Shawnetta. Oh well. A rose by any other name might still want to get freaky with me.

"Nice to meet you, Shawnetta." I smiled back and watched the smoke escape from her red, pouty lips.

Mr. Unlucky Deuce was complaining sourly to another old guy at the next table while I started stacking up my chips and getting them out of the way for the next hand. "Four goddamn deuces. Goddamn rolled-up trips from the git-go. Slow-played it, had 'em all reeled in nice and right, and then bang. Skinny dude gets a goddamn royal. Goddamn it. I got no goddamn luck at all."

Two security guards and the poker room manager walked up to me. The manager smiled and extended his hand. "Congratulations on your win, Mr. . . . ?"

"Carey." I shook his hand happily. "Drew Carey." I was waiting for him to offer me a free meal or a room, or some other big-winner extra that I've always heard about but never had. Hey, a room here would be great! It would save me and Shawnetta a walk.

"Yes, congratulations, Mr. Carey," he smiled. The security guards inched just a little closer. "Now, forgive me for asking," he said uncomfortably, "but may I see some ID please?"

I was two months short of my twenty-first birthday. Therefore, I was illegally loitering in the casino. As they walked me out, I saw my pile of chips being pushed toward Mr. Deuce, who had the next highest hand. He looked like he'd just been saved by Jesus. Maybe he had.

The guards left me on the sidewalk outside the Horseshoe. They felt bad for me and said so. Everyone in the poker room did except for Mr. Deuce. It was one of the wildest hands of poker anyone had seen in a long time.

Shawnetta had gotten up from the table right before I was asked to leave, and was waiting for me as I passed near the poker machines by the door. She was with a tall blonde who was, frankly, butt ugly. Big nose, thick glasses, fat hips. She was wearing nice clothes, but they would've looked better hanging on the rack back at the store.

When Shawnetta saw me, she whispered something to her friend and they both walked slowly toward me, smiling. God, she had strong legs. I'd bet they'd feel great wrapped around me. Maybe her friend could join us. I could put up with the ugly one as long as Shawnetta was there, too.

"Hello, Drew," she said, huskily. "Sorry about what happened at the table. Why, that was just *awful*," she pouted.

"Yeah," I smiled, trying to act unconcerned. "Missed it by two months. Who's your pretty friend?"

"Oh, this is my good girlfriend Jeanelle," she said. Jeanelle blushed. "We thought we'd take you out for a little drink, help you get over what happened to you back there." She stepped in closer, letting her breasts brush against me and locking my eyes to hers.

"You poor, poor, thing," she whispered, raising one eyebrow. Her lips were an inch from mine and I could feel the heat from her breath. I got the message special delivery. I took her face in my hand and kissed her, hard.

"Ohhh, darlin'!" Shawnetta squealed as she wiggled in my arms. "We are gonna have *such* a good time! Aren't we, Jeanelle?" Jeanelle smiled at me and licked her lips. Gross. But the way Shawnetta was running her hands over me I didn't care. "Maybe we can even get a little rough with you, huh, you skinny little thing? You like it a little rough?" She grabbed me through my pants.

"Yeah," I breathed. "Yeah, maybe I do." My God, she made my motor run. I grabbed her tight ass and gave it a squeeze, pressing myself against her muscular thigh to let her know how much horsepower I had. She pressed back. "The rougher the better," I said, nibbling at her ear and kissing her again. I'd never picked up a woman this fast. Maybe today was my lucky day after all.

I had one more thing I wanted to do before I went with Shawnetta and her repulsive friend. The video poker machines were right off the sidewalk, just a couple of feet away from us.

One of the security guards still had his eye on me and I wanted to show them that I could still gamble whenever I felt like it and there was nothing that they, or their stupid laws could do.

I held up one of the last quarters I had so he could see it. "Too young to gamble, huh?" I sneered, and dropped it into the machine. "Well, screw you. How do you like that, ya stupid rent-a-cop, ya?"

As the security guards came up to me, I hit the deal button and almost had a heart attack. I'd drawn another royal flush, all diamonds. With only one stinking quarter in. The machine started clanging and whooping and spitting out sixty-two dollars and fifty cents worth of quarters. Sixty-two more dollars (and fifty cents) that I should've got to keep but didn't. The only bright side was that if I had put in five quarters, it would have been a thousand.

"Buddy, you got the worst luck I've ever seen in my life," one of the security guards said, sincerely, as they escorted me, Shawnetta, and Jeanelle to the door.

Looking back, I don't know if he was so right. After all, I did get two royal flushes in one day. The very same day I was overpowered in a cheap motel room by a pair of sex-crazed transvestites.

How lucky could one guy get?

TACKLING
JIM BROWN

Larry Moore was the most pathetic person I knew. He was also one of the only people I knew to ever get on TV. What he did to get on TV was so spectacularly stupid, even for Larry, that none of us could believe it. Still can't, really. Once in a while, when we're drinking, someone will say, "Remember what happened to Larry when . . . ?" Of course, I remember without even being asked. I remember every time it rains.

We weren't getting along so well back then, because he suspected that I had pushed him out the window of my house while we were both naked. I did, but good luck proving it in court. I told him that he fell, and he was so drunk and hurting at the time he had no choice but to believe me.

I had a good reason to do it, and he only suffered a broken arm and a couple of cracked ribs, but the fact that we were both naked when it happened started a lot of nasty rumors around the neighborhood. Of course, none of *those* rumors were true.

I don't want to get into the whole reason why he was naked, but I was naked to make cleaning up the blood easier after I stabbed him. Which I didn't. I just pushed him out the window. You'd think he'd be grateful.

Larry had been drinking heavily up until "his fall," as he called it, but now, he was in a rehab program at Deaconess Hospital that he got into through his mom's insurance. He was back living in the basement of his parents' house. I heard he was still drinking.

The rehab program at Deaconess was cosponsored by the Cleveland Cares Foundation; a bunch of mushy-headed do-gooders that believed that no one was responsible for their own actions anymore. People at the meetings would actually get up and say, "Hi, I'm so-and-so, and society has made me an alcoholic."

On this particular weekend in November, Larry, along with a couple of other of the rehab honor students, was given a free field pass to see the Browns, led by star quarterback Bernie Kosar. It was some kind of community outreach thing by the Browns to reward people for being social outcasts and drunks. Leave it to an NFL owner to see nothing wrong with being rewarded for having a losing record.

I happened to be at the same game with my friends Jerry and Brian, but since we were just hardworking taxpayers, we had to buy our own tickets. We then traded them to a scalper, along with some extra cash, for seats that were just thirty rows up behind the Browns bench.

"Why are we paying this extra money?" Jerry protested as we made our way past the scalper and toward the gate. "The seats we had were fine."

"Yeah," Brian agreed. "And we're going to listen to it on the radio anyway, so what's the difference where we sit?"

I held up the expensive pair of Bushnell binoculars that used to belong to my father before he died. "Look," I said, waving them around, "I'm not going to sit in fucking row double-Z, okay? I want to see a football game, not an ant farm. Besides, Larry's down on the field today, remember? I don't want to take any chances of missing anything. If I'm lucky, he might get hit in the head by an overthrown pass or get knocked over during a tackle." God, I hated that guy. He had cost me my job *and* my girlfriend, and I would've pushed him out of a window every day if I could. Naked, if I had to.

We headed straight to gate A, and as soon as we got inside the stadium we felt it. It was a feeling we had talked about many times, late at night, in hushed, reverent tones over coffee and cigarettes. A feeling that we only got when we were inside the hallowed walls of the great Cleveland Municipal Stadium. The feeling of History. The idea that it had been there forever, and would always be there for the city of Cleveland to enjoy. Our grandfathers had watched games there, our fathers, and now us. We would take our children there, and they would take their children. It was the only structure in the city that gave you that feeling. It was the magnificent grand dame of Cleveland sports, and I was filled with pride every time I saw it.

Most of the greatest moments in Cleveland sports history had happened there. And not just for the Browns. Even the Cleveland Indians had a couple of highlights.

I was there in a box seat with my brother Roger for Dennis Eckersly's no-hitter. A year later he was traded. And when the Indians named Frank Robinson as the first black manager in baseball history, I was there with Roger for opening day. Frank was a player/manager, which you don't see anymore of these days, and he hit a home run off the first pitch in his first at bat. He was also the first black manager to be fired just over a year later. There was also the famous "Beer Night Riot" when the Indians played the Texas Rangers and decided to sell twelve-ounce plastic cups of beer for a dime. People couldn't drink the stuff fast enough and ended up brawling on the field with the players. Roger and I missed that night, but Jerry was there and got hit in the head with an empty wine bottle. Because of that, for one afternoon, he was the coolest kid in our high school.

Most of the great memories in Municipal Stadium were courtesy of the Browns. The Cleveland Browns: the winningest team in the history of the NFL, if you counted all the games they played in the 1940s, which we did. Although my favorite Browns moment had nothing to do with the team itself. It came to mind as my friends and I walked through the turnstiles and down the giant cement walkway to our section, the smell of winter and warm hot dogs filling the air.

I remember that it was really snowy and cold out that great day in Brown's history, and a photographer had been knocked unconscious after being run over by a wide receiver and a defensive back who were fighting over an incomplete touchdown pass. Because of where he was hit, half of his body was lying in the end zone and they had to stop the game while the paramedics looked after him.

The crowd couldn't stand the thought of the game being stopped for one minute, especially over a photographer, so they started throwing snowballs at him while he lay half-dead, facedown in the snow. Snowball after snowball just rained down on this poor sonuvabitch, and were even bouncing off the paramedics, who looked like they were going to need paramedics of their own if it kept up.

I was watching the game from home that day, and the TV announcers were shocked, just shocked, at the rowdy behavior of the Browns fans.

I wasn't shocked, though. I was laughing my ass off.

Maybe the same thing will happen to that asshole Larry, I thought, smiling, as I jostled my way down the row to my seat.

As I adjusted my official WMMS/Browns seat cushion and got out my Magic 105.7/Browns hand warmer (half the Browns stuff we had was from some radio station giveaway), I could just imagine him: Larry being handed his ticket and field credentials. Larry walking through the same tunnel that the players got to walk through. Larry smelling the fresh grass of Cleveland Municipal Stadium while I'm up here in the clouds sitting on cold wooden slats. Larry getting creamed by a linebacker and being knocked out of his dirty brown loafers, the blood seeping through his black Member's Only jacket as he lay there, disheveled and unconscious.

I knew that's what he'd be wearing from when we used to be friends. They were part of his "lucky Browns outfit," which consisted of everything that he owned that was orange or brown, Cleveland's official colors. Besides the brown loafers, he also would always wear a Browns sweatshirt that he got at a swap meet for ten dollars, orange knit pants with brown pockets that were too short and too tight, and orange socks. His Member's Only jacket was always left open to show off the logo on the sweatshirt, no matter how cold it was or how hard the wind was blowing.

I adjusted my binoculars and looked for him while the teams

went through their warm-ups. It didn't take me long to find him. He looked like a big, fat, hairy orange safety cone with brown spots.

"Aw, Jesus, look at him," I muttered to Jerry and Brian. Larry and his fellow miscreants were being introduced to David Modell, the vice president of the Cleveland Browns and son of the owner, Art Modell. "Hi, Mr. Modell!" I mocked Larry's voice as he shook David Modell's hand. "Thanks for everything you've done for Cleveland! How do you like my pants?"

Then, suddenly, I saw Him. The best running back in the history of the Cleveland Browns. The finest NFL running back ever. NFL record holder. Hall of Famer. Community activist. The greatest, hustlin'est, baddest sonuvabitch to ever play the game. Jim Brown, a.k.a God.

Jim Brown was waved over by David Modell. Oh, no. Goddamn it! Stupid Larry is going to get to meet Jim Brown. Jesus! I'm stuck up here in the almost cheap seats, and that idiot gets to shake hands with the greatest running back that ever played the game because he's in a rehab program? Fuck. Damn it.

Yeah, go ahead and smile, you dummy. Like Jim Brown could care. The only thing he'll ever remember about you is your moron pants.

I mocked him some more. "Ooohh, Jim Brown shook my hand! And he was huge! Just huge! Yeah, he was in great shape. No gut. No gut at all. Oh yeah, real polite. Couldn't believe it. Signed my shirt! Look! J-i-m B-r-o-w-n!" Dope. Jerk off. Girlfriend stealer.

I passed the binoculars to Jerry and Brian. I didn't need to see a close-up of this travesty.

Jim Brown had just excused himself and was walking away from the group of rejects. His back was turned.

"Hey, he's got a little bit of a limp there," Jerry noticed through the lenses.

"Yeah, well no kidding," Brian added. "The way he used to get hit? I wouldn't even be able to walk at all."

"Uh oh," Jerry said.

"Uh oh?" I asked. "Uh oh what?"

"Here, look," he said, shoving the binoculars at me. "Do you see what I'm seeing?"

Jim Brown was walking away from the players area where David Modell was entertaining the rehab rangers. He limped slightly, but his walk was steady and proud. This was the field were he spent the best playing days of his life, where he set all of his records. He was like an old lion in the jungle, king of all he surveyed.

Larry, the stupid fat guy in the orange pants, was staring at him with his mouth open. He wasn't paying attention to the rest of the group at all. I adjusted the lenses slightly to bring his face into better focus.

He hadn't shaved, which didn't surprise me, and even though his bright orange knit Browns cap was pulled down past his eyebrows, I could still tell that he was puzzled by something, that he was working something out. Then, I saw his eyes widen into a strange look of awareness and he started to scream.

I lowered the binoculars so I could take in the entire tableau without missing anything. And what I saw was Larry Moore, the biggest loser I knew, run screaming up from behind Jim Brown, the greatest NFL running back ever, and tackle him from behind.

And what a tackle it was. Vicious and cowardly, it blindsided the great Jim Brown, snapping him backward and sending him flying into the frozen ground with Larry wrapped around him like three fat, badly dressed linebackers. No one could believe it.

The expensive Bushnell binoculars that were handed down

to me by my dear dead father fell from my fingers and broke. Brian dropped his beer. All three of us shot out of our seats, and with the rest of the fans in Cleveland Municipal Stadium, cried out "Whatthefuckwasthat?!"

Larry leaped to his feet and started *jumping up and down* with his arms raised victoriously in the air, like he had done something great. Like he was actually happy that he had delivered such a cheap shot to the legendary Jim Brown.

The local TV stations showed it every half hour for the rest of the day.

"We interrupt this program for this breaking news. A westside man viciously attacked beloved retired Cleveland Browns running back Jim Brown today as he stood on the sidelines before a game at Municipal Stadium, tackling him from behind when he wasn't looking."

Then they showed the tackle, in slow motion, and Larry jumping up and down in his dippy orange pants. When his arms were raised, his Member's Only jacket and sweatshirt got pulled up so that his hairy belly showed. Cut to: Jim Brown lying dazed in the frozen tundra for a full five seconds before he jumped up and started looking around for the fool who'd laid hands on him.

"As a precautionary measure, Jim Brown was taken to Cleveland Metro Hospital where he was examined and released." Then, more video: Jim Brown being shoved down the hospital hallway by the cops.

"I don't need any (beep!) hospital, (beep!)'n (beep!)! Let me go! I'll kill that (beep! beep! beep!)! I'll kill him! I'll kill him! (beep!)"

"The suspect, who seemed deranged, was tentatively identified by police as Larry Moore, a lifelong Cleveland resident and graduate of James Ford Rhodes High School. He was immediately arrested and charged with assault." A shot of Larry's rehab ID picture appeared in the corner of the screen as they showed a group of five or six Cleveland policemen trying to keep Jim Brown away from him.

"Details on the Eyewitness News On Five at Eleven, followed by the Sunday Night Movie."

"*Seems* deranged?" I guffawed into my beer.

"One can short of a six-pack," chuckled Jerry as he lit a cigarette.

"Fucking goof ball if you ask me," added Brian. "I never did like him."

We kept drinking and telling Larry stories until the eleven o'clock news came on. Larry was the lead story, along with his picture and the news that he had already made bail. They called him "The Most Hated Man In Cleveland," a title he would hold until Art Modell decided to move the Browns to Baltimore for fifty million dollars.

I walked home that night feeling no pain. It was a happy kind of drunk. The kind of drunk you get when your team wins the game, or at a wedding when you're still single.

I had just turned the corner onto my street when I walked across my . . .

Door? The front door to my house was lying in the middle of the sidewalk. What the hell? Seeing your front door lying in the middle of the sidewalk at the end of your street is like seeing a fish driving a car, or a flying pig.

I didn't know what to do. I figured, "Hey, it's my door. I better take it home with me." It was a struggle to lift it up and balance it on my head and walk it back to my house. My buzz went away faster than that guy who did "Achey Breaky Heart." Can't think of his name right now. Damn, that thing was heavy.

Farther down the block, I saw my front porch swing busted into pieces on Mrs. Franklin's tree lawn. I decided to leave it there, since I was tired from carrying the door, and Mrs. Franklin didn't like me anyway, ever since I did such a lousy job of mowing her lawn that one summer.

When I got to my house a minute later, it looked like it had been used as a demonstration for a vandalism class. Windows were broken, the carpet was torn out and pulled halfway out of the entrance where the front door used to be, and rude, threatening messages were spray-painted all over the aluminum siding. Sign, sign, everywhere a sign. Blockin' up the scenery, messin' my mind. FUCK YOU LARRY MOORE! Can't you read the sign?

They thought that Larry still lived here.

Of course. This was his last address before he went into rehab, after I pushed him out of my second-floor window. Someone got the address from the rehab center at Deaconess Hospital and came looking for him.

I knocked on my neighbor's door to use the phone because mine had been ripped out of the wall. If I had been home they probably would've shoved it up my ass. Naturally, my neighbor never heard or saw a thing.

I got hold of my brother Roger and made arrangements to stay over at his place, and then went down to the basement to get a couple of sheets of poster board that I had stored there and some paint.

I made up a sign that said, LARRY MOORE DOES NOT LIVE HERE—PLEASE LEAVE ME ALONE, and nailed it to the front of the house. Next to it, just in case any of the brothers from the east side decided they wanted to come around for a piece of the action, I nailed up another sign that said, BLACK OWNED.

★   ★   ★

The next day, Brian and Jerry came over to help me clean up. None of the neighbors came out to help, although I did see a couple of them peeking out from behind their curtains. We were in the kitchen having a beer break when Larry came limping out of the spare bedroom in what was left of his lucky Browns outfit. His jaw was swollen and his eyes were a deep black and blue. His clothes were torn, there were scratches and bruises all over his arms, and he smelled like he had shit himself.

"Hey guys," he said, as if nothing had happened.

I jumped about a foot in the air and swore. "Where the hell were you!" I screamed at him. "What the fuck did you let happen to my house??!!" I lunged at him but Jerry and Brian held me back.

"Take it easy, Drew, take it easy," Larry said casually, and then "Holy moly . . . what happened in here? I heard them doing a lot of bangin' around, but man . . ."

"You prick! You asshole!" I was screaming at the top of my lungs trying to get to him. I didn't know Brian and Jerry were that strong.

"Hey, hey, keep it down!" Jerry warned me. It was all he and Brian could do to keep me pinned to the far wall. "Do you want everyone to know he's here?" That took a lot of the fight out of me. If a mob was still looking for him and found him here, we'd be as dead as he was.

"What are you doing here? What happened?" I demanded, barely able to contain myself.

"Well," Larry said calmly, sitting down where the kitchen table would've been if it wasn't already laying broken in two in the side yard, "it's like this . . ."

My house was the first place Larry knew to run to after he got his bail, since I took such good care of him before when he was "sick" (his word for lazy and drunk). That was good news and bad news. The good news was that he really did believe me when I told him that his trip out of my window was caused by a fall and not a push, and the bad news was that he thought I still liked him enough to help him.

He had called his parents, but they had already disowned him. His father actually said "Son? I have no son," before he slammed the phone down in Larry's ear.

Then he decided to walk over to my house, got followed by one guy, then two, then a whole mob. They tore up the house looking for him, and then beat him senseless, leaving him in the spare bedroom to die.

"Well, serves you right, you dick. What's the big idea tackling Jim Fucking *Brown*," I could barely stop myself from shouting, "in the middle of Cleveland Municipal fucking STADIUM!? *Huh!?*" Larry had no answer, and could only hang his head like a scolded child. "Why didn't you just go over to Hough and take a shit on a picture of Martin Luther King while you were at it? Or burn the flag during the Fourth Of July picnic over at the VFW hall?"

I should've stabbed him when I had the chance. Why did my church ever drill "Thou shalt not kill" into my head with people like Larry walking around?

"I didn't think he was a real guy," Larry said softly. "I just thought he was Jim Brown, a guy on TV. Even after he shook my hand I couldn't believe it. I wanted to know what it felt like to tackle a guy on TV like I'd seen so many times, and since I didn't think he was a real person, I did it."

"You didn't think it was a real person? Even though he was standing right in front of you?" Brian asked. "So that made it okay to tackle him?"

"Yeah," Larry said.

We were silent for a moment, taking it all in.

"How'd it feel?" Jerry asked quietly.

"Fucking great, man. I tackled Jim Brown."

"Well," Brian pulled a cigarette from his shirt. "That makes sense."

None of us spoke for the next few minutes. I had to get rid of Larry before he got us all killed. I would've called the police, but then I might end up on the news as the guy that harbored the guy who hurt Jim Brown. It's bad enough that one mob already thought so, I didn't need the whole city getting the news. Besides, with the way my luck was going I would probably be charged with aiding and abetting an asshole, then gang-raped by every Jim Brown fan in county jail.

I looked over at Brian and Jerry. It was a natural habit of mine to crack sick jokes in times of personal disaster, and if there ever was such a time, it was now. "Hey Larry, maybe we should send you on tour, huh? I wonder how many fans you could make in Pittsburgh if you whacked Terry Bradshaw in the head with a baseball bat?"

"Yeah," Brian laughed, "especially if you did it in downtown Pittsburgh on Terry Bradshaw Day." More laughs from the three of us. Larry was the only one not joining in. I don't think Larry got it.

Jerry got up, cracked open a cold beer, and said, "After all the times that Terry Bradshaw and the fucking Steelers beat us in the seventies, I'd probably buy the guy that whacked him a six-pack. Maybe throw him a parade of his own. Heh heh heh . . ."

This time I was the one not laughing along. Jerry had the answer. People in Pittsburgh didn't care what happened to Jim Brown. They hated Jim Brown. Jim Brown was, well, a Brown. They were probably glad that someone nailed him. And even if they weren't it would still be okay.

Say a guy hates the Browns like everyone else in Pittsburgh does (and he's especially going to hate Jim Brown, even though they begrudgingly respect him because he was such a great player). He's not going to want to murder some social misfit like Larry who's done something to hurt the greatest Cleveland Brown who ever lived.

"Pack your shit, Larry," I announced. "I'm driving you to Pittsburgh."

"But," said Larry, "I don't have any shit to pack."

I quickly explained my plan to Brian and Jerry. They both agreed that Pittsburgh was the perfect place for someone as wretched and hated as Larry Moore.

"Don't worry, Larry," Brian assured him. "They got jobs in Pittsburgh. You'll find something. And in the meantime, you can sleep in a shelter, you know, The Salvation Army or something. Just until your leg heals up and you can get back on your feet."

"Yeah," Jerry said cheerily, patting Larry on the back and then immediately regretting it because of the cootie factor. "With your credentials, you could end up being the king of Pittsburgh someday."

They both promised to stay and watch the house while I was gone. It only takes a little over five hours to get to Pittsburgh and back from Cleveland, which isn't long, but I still didn't have a front door and didn't want any more damage done to the house.

Before Larry could start to think it out and argue with me, I threw an old dish towel over his head to cover his face, and herded him out of the back door to the garage.

Thankfully, the mob wasn't after anything valuable so my '82 Dodge Omni was still there. Larry was limping pretty bad as I hustled him over to the garage door. I think they might've broken his knee, but I didn't care. I was not only getting rid of a curse, I was getting rid of it permanently by dropping him in Pittsburgh. True, it was only a two-and-a-half hour drive, but for people like Larry, that's half way around the world. I would never see this walking happiness repellent again.

"But I don't want to go to Pittsburgh," Larry whined, as I pushed him, blind and lame, into the small front seat of the Dodge.

"Shut up and get in the car, jinx," I told him, and slammed the door as hard as I could.

Our first stop was one I didn't want to make just yet, but the gas tank was almost empty and I'm sure we wouldn't have made it to the Ohio Turnpike. I didn't want to get stuck hitchhiking with Larry while I was still in Jim Brown country.

The closest gas station was a SuperAmerica on the corner of Ridge and Brookpark, about a block from I-480. Then it was 480 to 77, 77 to the Ohio Turnpike, which turns into the Pennsylvania Turnpike, and then we'd both be free men. It had been snowing, but the streets were clear and the salt had melted away the icy patches on the road, so I would be able to go as fast as I could get away with.

"Can I take this dish rag off of my face?" Larry whimpered. "It smells."

"No. Shut up before I make you eat it."

"C'mon, man. It stinks."

"No! Not until we're out of Cleveland. Now shut up."

"C'mon."

"No."

I turned on the radio and turned it up as loud as it could go, which wasn't very. The speakers crackled, and it sounded like we were listening to music through a paper cup at the end of a string. Only loud, which was the important thing.

"Fuck you, man, I'm taking it off," Larry yelled over the radio, and he whipped the dish towel off of his head and threw it out of the window. I punched him while I drove.

"You idiot! You freakin' idiot!" Punch! Punch! Punch! "You're gonna get us both killed if someone sees you! We're only in a Dodge Omni! We couldn't outrun a kid on a skate-board!" Punch!

"Ow! Ow! Ow! Ow!"

"Put your head in your hands! Put your head in your hands!" Punch! Punch! Punch!

We had only driven two blocks.

It was the middle of the afternoon and the SuperAmerica was packed. Bright orange banners with GO BROWNS!" written on them were strung all over between the gas pumps and the main building, where the windows were painted with caricatures of Bernie Kosar and Eric Metcalf. Larry had his face in his hands and was crying. I grabbed his head and pushed it down between his legs.

"Listen, Larry. I don't want to hurt you. I—quit squirming! I don't want to hurt you!"

"You're going to kill me!"

"No. No Larry. I'm not going to kill you, now settle down. Settle down." I softened my voice to assure him, without loosening my grip. "You know SuperAmerica with all of the Browns banners everywhere?" I asked him.

Larry went limp.

"That's right. That's where we are now. Keep your head down while I get gas. I'm not fooling, Larry. If I so much as see your face, I'm going to throw you out of the car right here." Larry sobbed softly.

"Can you get me some smokes?" he asked meekly.

"Sure Larry, what kind?" I was friendly now. I was the bad cop, now I'm the good cop.

"Marlboro Lights 100's. In the box."

"Yeah, whatever," I told him, and got out of the car to pump the gas.

SuperAmerica was one of those pain-in-the-ass gas stations where you had to pay first before you pumped. I had to walk out of my car, through the cold and wind, wait in line, pay the overworked cashier, walk back through the cold and wind, pump my gas, walk back for my change, and then back to my car. All because my credit wasn't good enough to get one of their stupid charge cards and pay-at-the-pump technology hadn't been invented yet.

It was after I gave the cashier a twenty and was on the second leg of the relay that I noticed the crowd gathering by the stacked jugs of wiper fluid. Larry had gotten out of the car and put the hose in the gas tank for me, trying to be helpful. He waved to me as I walked toward him, smiling through his swollen jaw and loose teeth.

"I'll pump, you pay!" he yelled across the lot.

"Larry! Get in the car, Larry!" I ran toward the car as fast as I could.

Someone in the crowd yelled, "I knew that was that motherfucker! Get him! Jim Brown! Jim Brown!" and they all came after us like a swarm of angry bees.

I was the first one in the car and already had it started when the first of the mob jumped on my hood. Fuck Larry. I'm gone.

"Jim Brown! Jim Brown!" the mob yelled. They were all over the car in a flash, and were banging on the windshield and trunk, trying to rip the car apart like a can of tuna.

Larry, who in spite of his injuries was still pretty fast, threw his upper body into the open window of the car before I could peel out, and was yelling, "Go! Go! Go! Go! For the love of God! They've got my leg! Arrrrrrgghhh!!!! Oh, Jesus! Arrggggh!!!"

I gunned the car out of the parking lot, snapping the head of the gas hose out and sending 87 octane spattering all over the asphalt. I thanked God that I had wired the muffler to the bumper last week, or the sparks would've gotten us all blown to smithereens.

Larry was still upside down in the seat with his legs dangling out of the window thirty seconds later when I fishtailed my Omni onto 480 and hauled ass to the turnpike. His pants leg was torn off at the knee, and both his shoes were gone.

"Ahhh, my knee. My knee . . . oh, God . . ." he moaned.

"Did they get your good knee, or was it the bad knee?" I asked.

"The bad knee . . . oh, my God . . . ughhnnn . . ."

Damn, I thought. I was hoping they got to both of them.

Larry had managed to pump in just over a quarter of a tank before the mob attacked us, so I settled in for a nice quiet ride to the Pittsburgh border. I could wait to fill the tank until we were out of Ohio and into Pennsylvania, where it would be safe.

And, other than the woman that worked in the toll booth spitting at us (but on me), it was finally starting to be a pleasant trip. Larry was silent, except for the occasional moan, which I was getting used to, and we listened to National Public Radio without having to talk to each other.

We were halfway to Youngstown, when Larry turned to me and said, "I'm sorry about Natalie."

My eyes flashed with anger, and I immediately went back to

the moment that I caught them in bed together. In *my* bed.
"Yeah. She was nice. Oh well."

"No," he said, "I mean I'm sorry I, you know . . ."

"No, I don't know," I seethed.

"Well, you know, I don't want to say it in front of you."

"Say what?!" I yelled. "That you fucked her?! That you
fucked her right in front of me in my own bed?!!" I hit the
steering wheel with my fist.

"Yeah. Pretty much that."

I was furious. What was he thinking, bringing that up at a
time like this? What was he ever thinking when he did anything? I was in love with her, and she loved me more. She told
me so.

He continued, "I just thought, you know, if you knew how
special things were between us back then that you'd understand." He sighed and looked up at the roof of the car. "We
were on a really spiritual trip, you know? It's like, we were
feeling each other's souls or something. She was like this . . .
sunshine that I'd been waiting for. I mean, I really dug her, you
know? I wanted to spend the rest of my life with her."

You really dug her? Well, far out. Like, she told everyone she
only slept with you for fun because you had a huge dick, so the
laugh's on you.

I didn't say anything, though. I couldn't. I had tried to forget
Natalie, but now my mind was filled with her. Her face, her
touch, her laugh. All gone. Because of Larry. Larry and his big
dick, and my bad timing. Larry saw that I was ready to start
crying.

"Aww, man," he put his hand on my shoulder. "It's okay,
it's okay." I stiffened up and ignored him. "C'mon, man. Give
me a hug."

"What!?" I sat up straight. "No! Get off me!"

"Just one hug, man. You'll feel better."

Punch!

"Ow!"

It was fifteen minutes before Larry had the nerve to speak to me again. "Uh, hey man, can we stop for some smokes? I'm really dying for a cigarette right now."

Oh really? Well, suffer, bitch.

"All right," I sighed. "There's a rest stop coming up in a couple of miles. We're almost out of gas anyway."

Even though we were still in Ohio, we were well out of Cleveland by now so I figured it would be okay if Larry showed his face. I pulled into the first pump I found, and got out to stretch.

"C'mon, Larry. You can get out now. It's safe." I even managed a smile now. "I think you can even go inside and hit the john if you want to."

"You know what, man," he said as he leaned out of the window, "my leg's really killing me. I don't think I can walk on it. I mean, my knee's really swollen."

I wasn't about to start feeling sorry for him now. "Okay, then. You pump, I'll pay."

"Hey," he called out as I walked away. "Don't forget my smokes, all right? Marlboro Lights 100's in the box! All right?"

Yeah, whatever. Cigarettes. You want cigarettes.

I paid for the gas, took a leak, bought a Pepsi, and was enjoying a leisurely stroll back out to the car when a young kid in a Browns parka stopped me. He was with a couple of other unfriendly-looking punks. He smiled at me, but I knew he didn't mean it.

"Hey dude," he said, "me and my friends are trying to figure out something and we were wondering if you could help us."

I was already worried, but tried not to show it. "Uh, sure man, what's up?" I said, trying to keep my voice steady.

The tough kid jerked a thumb over to where Larry was standing. He had already finished pumping the gas, and was leaning against the car with his arms crossed in his fruity orange pants and orange socks with no shoes. "Ain't that the dude from the news? The one that tackled Jim Brown?"

"Who him?" I squeaked. And then, clearing my throat. "Ha ha. Man, no way. He's a big Browns fan. He'd never do something like that. I mean, look at his pants."

The kid looked at me and let his head tilt to the side while his eyebrows scrunched together in thought.

"Well, see ya!" I said to him, and walked as quickly as I could to the car.

"Larry!" I hissed, trying not to attract attention. "Larry! Get in the car!"

"Ya got my smokes?" Larry asked, agitated.

"Oh, for cryin' out loud," I muttered, and flipped him the pack that I'd bought.

"Hey man, these are menthols. Camel Light menthols."

"So? Get in the car! Let's go! I think somebody saw you."

"And they're in a soft pack. They're not even in a box. They're Camel Light menthols in a soft pack. I need Marlboro Light 100's in a box."

I looked back to see how close the three kids were to us. They were gone. Thank God.

"Who gives a shit what cigarettes you smoke? They're free, aren't they? Just get in the car."

"Look," Larry said forcefully. "I'm tired of you pushing me around already. I can't hardly walk, I don't have no clothes, my shoes are missing, and you talk to me like I'm your slave or something. And now, all I want is a simple pack of cigarettes, and you're shitting on me again. Well, I've had it."

"Larry, just get in the car, huh? We're almost there and—"

"I WANT MY FUCKING CIGARETTES, MOTHER-FUCKER! GIMME MY CIGARETTES!"

Anybody who's ever lived with a smoker will know that they consider this a reasonable request. But, still, I was stunned.

"You want your cigarettes?" I told him. "Well, fucking buy your own, then. You can fucking walk to fucking Pittsburgh for all I care." Then I jumped in my car and stared at the empty ignition slot where my keys were hanging before I went in to pay for the gas. Larry leaned down and dangled them into the passenger-side window.

"Marlboro Lights 100's. In the box. It's very important."

I was tired of arguing. I got out of the car and started walking back inside. Give the big baby what he wants and let's get the hell out of here, that's what I'll do. The sooner he's in Pittsburgh the better as far as I'm concerned. And hey, aren't those the nice young men I saw loitering outside before coming my way? And who are those people with them? And what are those things they're carrying?

Uh oh.

I turned and ran, but this time I didn't make it. Neither did Larry. I remember trying to fool them by screaming, "Yeah! That's the guy that dissed our man! Let's fuck him up! Jim Brown! Jim Brown!" And I would've helped them, too, except someone hit me in the base of my neck with something big and heavy, and I went down to the pavement.

I remember being kicked in the ribs, and having my legs jumped on. Then I remember waking up by the trash bins at the rest stop with Larry, and checking myself for damage.

Face, okay. Whew. They stayed away from the face. My head hurt though. Probably from the whack to the back of my neck. Legs sore, but functioning. Feels like they're just bruised. Ribs very sore. Might have to get those X-rayed. My left shoulder had been bent into some weird shape that you couldn't even put a Ken doll into, and I couldn't move my arm at all. Probably from when they dragged me here. (It's okay now, though. And, I can tell you when a twister's coming.)

Larry was really bad off. They left his legs alone, but only because I don't think they knew he had a bad knee. He was one big bruise, and his eyes were just slits from being pounded so much. His lips were swollen, and he was bleeding from his ear.

And, of course, since it involved Larry, no one saw a thing. No one sees a fat guy in bright orange pants and his friend getting the shit kicked out of them at a busy turnpike rest stop.

By the time I got my slashed tires replaced and got going again, it was almost ten at night when we drove by exit four of the Pennsylvania Turnpike. Close enough to Pittsburgh for me. I pulled the car off to the side of the road.

"Here ya go, Larry. Out." He didn't argue. He was too tired and beaten at this point to try.

I left him like that. Beaten to within an inch of his life. No shoes, one orange sock. Tight knit orange pants with one leg torn away and the back pockets ripped out so that you could see his underwear. An old Browns sweatshirt and a ripped Member's Only jacket. Standing at the side of the Pennsylvania Turnpike near exit four, shivering in the snow.

"Hey, thanks for the lift, buddy!" he called to me, waving. "I think I'm gonna be all right here. I do. I think I'm really gonna like Pittsburgh!"

Was I happy or sad? Did I learn a lesson from our journey together? Was I a better man because of it?

No.

I drove off without looking back.

"Good-bye, you idiot."